Craft Lessons

Teaching Writing K–8

Second Edition

Ralph Fletcher
JoAnn Portalupi

Stenhouse Publishers
Portland, Maine

Stenhouse Publishers
www.stenhouse.com

Library of Congress Cataloging-in-Publication Data
Fletcher, Ralph J.
Craft lessons : teaching writing K–8 / Ralph Fletcher, JoAnn Portalupi. — 2nd ed.
    p. cm.
    Includes bibliographical references and index.
    ISBN 978-1-57110-706-0 (alk. paper)
    1. English language—Composition and exercises—Study and teaching (Elementary) 2. Creative writing (Elementary education) I. Portalupi, JoAnn. II. Title.
LB1576.F476 2007
372.62'3044—dc22   2007033883

Cover design by Catherine Hawkes, Cat & Mouse
Typesetting by Martha Drury

Manufactured in the United States of America on acid-free, recycled paper
13 12 11 10 09 08   9 8 7 6 5 4 3 2

To Philippa Stratton,
friend and editor extraordinaire,
who has put many fine professional books
into the hands of teachers.

We are honored to work with her.

Contents

Craft Lessons Organized by Subject

K–2 lessons appear between pages 16 and 51; grades 3–4 between pages 52 and 87; and grades 5–8 between pages 88 and 123. Some lessons are listed under more than one subject heading below.

Acknowledgments

Writing a new edition is a complex weave, an intricate braid of stuff from the original book with new material and new design elements. It took the entire Stenhouse team to complete this new project, especially Cathy Hawkes, Jay Kilburn, and Erin Trainer.

Our editor, Philippa Stratton, played conductor for this sometimes difficult project. She did her usual magnificent job, pulling together all the various elements into one cohesive whole.

Pat Johnson, a veteran reading teacher in Fairfax County, VA, and author of *One Child at a Time* (2006), made a significant contribution to this book. "Aunt Pat," along with Virginia teachers Tania Dedham, Kara Conques, and Katie Keier, read all the new material. The opportunity for us to see our writing and thinking through their eyes was enormously helpful.

We always cast a wide net—to teachers, colleagues, students—when we write our professional books. This book is no different. Many teachers provided helpful insight and suggestions for the new edition including Max Brand, Sue Carter, Kathleen Fay, Jan Furuta, Julie Leal, and Suzanne Whaley. Thanks to Mike McCormick, Pat Meehan, Randy Methuen, and Lisa Siemens.

Special thanks go to Aimee Buckner, Sue Carter, Lynn Herschlein, Franki Sibberson, and Michele Sodergren.

Several teachers kindly sent student writing samples. We are grateful to Ng Silvana and the teachers at PS 1—Sue Blais, Laurie McMahan, Karen McMichael, Jody Chang, and Anna Lee Lum.

Thanks to our friends and colleagues Martha Horn, Marianne Darr-Norman, and Cyrene Wells. Thanks to Artie Voigt and Dan Feigelson.

It has been a marvelous experience to watch our boys grow as individuals and as writers. Thanks to Taylor, Adam, Robert, and Joseph for keeping us grounded, for keeping it real.

We will forever be indebted to our dear friend Don Murray (1924–2006), the original craftsman. We will never forget you, Don.

Introduction

*I*f there's a book you want to read, but you can't find it, you've got to write it yourself. Novelist Toni Morrison said that, and we took it to heart. For years we had worked with teachers, helping them fine-tune their writing workshops. When it came to ideas for mini-lessons, teachers were ravenous; they couldn't get enough.

"Isn't there some kind of book of mini-lessons?" they asked. "Boy, could I use that now!"

When we wrote the first edition of *Craft Lessons*, we felt a measure of excitement (Here it is: The Secret Book of Mini-Lessons!) that was tempered with caution. Such a book would undoubtedly be useful to teachers, but we were also aware of potential dangers. We believed then, and still believe now, that skilled writing teachers need to become resourceful and self-reliant. Smart writing teachers learn how to "live off the land" by being responsive to all the unplanned teachable moments that arise during a writing workshop (Calkins 1986). In addition, we didn't want teachers to become reliant on any one-source, preprinted lesson materials.

Notes on This New Edition

After *Craft Lessons* was published in 1998, it quickly became a best seller. Since that time the world has changed in many ways, but one thing has not:

1

teachers everywhere continue to feel starved for time. In fact, with new curriculum mandates, daily specials, "pull-outs," and precious time devoted to test preparation, the situation has never been worse. That's why we believe that a book like *Craft Lessons*—a short, pithy, practical text—will continue to be useful for harried writing teachers.

In this new edition we have made a number of changes:

- We added seventeen brand-new craft lessons, most of which were drawn from teachers' comments about what needs they see in their students' writing.

- We made revisions on other craft lessons, swapping out mentor texts we use as models that have gone out of print for enduring titles that are in print, and are expected to stay in print for a long time.

- We included our latest thinking about teaching the elements of craft.

- We explained the role of the writer's notebook in helping students develop a sense of the writer's craft.

- We included thoughts about how these craft lessons fit into our newest thinking about the qualities of writing: Ideas, Design, Language, Presentation.

Kids in their first year of college often put on the "freshman fifteen." In a similar way, new editions of books like this one have a tendency to gain bulk, something we wanted to keep to a minimum. In updating this book we worked hard to strengthen it while maintaining its feel as a "lean-and-mean" resource for the diligent but harried writing teacher.

Writing as a Developmental Process

When it comes to the writer's craft, teachers often find themselves working in the dark. What are reasonable expectations for a first-grade writer? A fifth-grade writer? These questions rarely get answered in any satisfactory way. When they do get answered, we all breathe a sigh of relief.

Four first-grade teachers met to talk about writing. After about fifteen minutes, the talk moved to editing.

"What editing skills should you teach a first grader?" one teacher wondered aloud. "What's a reasonable expectation for a kid that age?"

"I'd say teach them ending punctuation: periods, question marks—punctuation," another teacher suggested. "And teach them to start the next sentence with a capital letter."

"Okay," the first teacher agreed. "But then what?"

After a moment's pause, the second teacher shrugged and replied: "Then they're ready for second grade."

Everybody laughed.

Writing is a developmental process, but the word *developmental* does not give a blank check for unlimited growth. First graders are not miniature college students. Experienced writing teachers understand this and don't introduce a skill like paragraphing until third or fourth grade. Rough developmental guidelines exist at every age, describing the range of what young writers can, and cannot, do.

This book explores what children can learn about the writer's craft as they become more sophisticated writers. Some of the questions we attempt to answer include: What behaviors are typical of first-grade writers? How can we help third graders focus their "bed-to-bed" narratives (stories that recount everything that happened from the time they got up to when they went to bed)? How might we best teach a fifth grader about the use of time in writing?

While we do not embrace a rigid scope-and-sequence of writing development, we do believe that writing teachers need to have a deep and profound knowledge of writing. This knowledge should include a sense of how writers grow as they move through the grades and move toward proficiency. We hope the information provided in this book serves that purpose.

Teaching Craft Lessons

We might visualize the writing process like this:

Conceive ⟶ Craft ⟶ Correct

It has been our sense that many teachers tend to interact with their students at the ends of the process—conceiving and correcting. Teachers show students how to use a variety of prewriting techniques (webs, story maps, time lines, and outlines). They give students detailed editing checklists to use, either individually or in pairs.

The item in the middle—craft—gets the least attention. During this part of the authoring cycle, students are left on their own to make a thousand decisions in their texts about leads, choice of verb, voice, structure, supporting detail, mood, character, and so forth. This is unfortunate because craft matters. Craft is the cauldron in which the writing gets forged.

Here's another way to envision the authoring cycle. You may have seen a similar diagram:

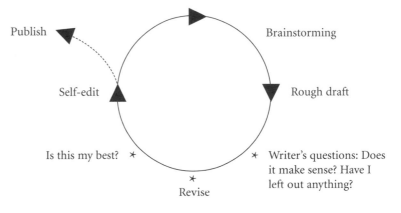

This all looks very nice and neat on paper. But it's no secret that most students pay scant attention to issues of craft (including revision) in the authoring cycle. Most young writers take a shortcut and move straight from the rough draft to publishing.

There are several reasons why students short-circuit this cycle. Writing is hard work. Writing involves not just one skill but a bundle of skills—sequencing, spelling, organizing, and so on. *Rereading* is one writing skill that too often gets overlooked. Don Murray once said, "I'm not a teacher of writing—I teach students how to reread their work." The writer's movement through the authoring cycle is driven by rereading. The three asterisks on the diagram above suggest places where it is crucially important for the writer to reread what he or she has written. If students don't know how to reread, we cannot expect them to have much luck crafting and recrafting their texts.

How This Book Is Organized

In *Craft Lessons* we try to break down vague language about craft. While writing this book we kept asking ourselves, How would we teach this particular craft element? What would we actually say to students? We pushed ourselves to find tangible ways to teach complex issues. We try to use language that is kid friendly and direct without being formulaic. The craft lessons found in this book come from our own teaching as well as our own writing. We have also drawn a few craft lessons from some wonderful writing teachers.

These craft lessons, however, cannot stand on their own. They will only thrive if they are rooted in classrooms that support writers. In the next chapter, "Setting the Table for Craft," we put forth essential conditions for creating classrooms that nurture young writers.

For the purposes of this book we have put students into three groups:

■ kindergarten through grade 2

■ grades 3 and 4

■ grades 5 through 8

As you'll see, we have designed craft lessons to meet the developmental needs of students in these three grade-level spans. Each section begins with a brief look at the characteristics writers typically display at each level. While we set out to describe the typical first-, third-, or sixth-grade writer, we all know that every child differs, and that students in any classroom span a wide range of abilities. You know your students best. While you may want to begin with the craft lessons that pertain to your grade level, we encourage you to read the lessons from the other sections as well. You're likely to find ideas that can be adapted to your own grade level. You may even find that a lesson from another section is just right for a particular student of yours.

We designed the craft lessons so each one follows the same consistent format:

- ■ **Discussion**—A brief look at the context for a particular craft lesson and the reasons for teaching it.

- ■ **How to Teach It**—Concrete language showing exactly how a teacher might bring this craft element to students. Most lessons are written using language that a teacher might actually use during a mini-lesson at the start of a writing workshop. The lessons can be taught just as well in an individual writing conference or in a small-group setting.

- ■ **Resource Material**—Here we list books or texts referred to in the craft lesson. Where possible, we have suggested additional texts that can be used to teach the craft lesson. At times we refer to a passage, poem, or piece of student writing that can be found in its entirety in the appendixes.

How you choose to use these lessons will have much to do with the needs of your students and the design of your writing classroom. After the craft lessons, you'll find a chapter titled "Questions and Answers," which explores ways you can make these craft lessons as meaningful/relevant as possible. We want this book to be practical. In that spirit, we confront predictable problems all of us encounter when working with young writers, and suggest our best ideas for extending the craft lessons.

While these craft lessons are meant to be indicative of what young writers are ready to learn, and how we might teach it to them, this book does not pretend to be comprehensive. In fact, many important issues of craft have been left out. Writing this book forced us to make many tough decisions. You won't find craft lessons that are specific to one particular genre (poetry, for instance).

Still, you will find more craft lessons than your students can reasonably absorb in one year. Amidst all the white noise about standards and writing rubrics, let's take a deep breath and be realistic: your students will not learn fifteen or twenty elements of craft during the year they spend with you. It makes more sense to choose a few issues you consider truly important to their growth as writers, lessons you believe they are ready to learn, and concentrate on those.

There's a tendency for all of us to get locked into our own perspectives. Kids see writing as a "school thing." Teachers may tend to see it as a "curriculum thing" (or a "testing thing"). It's far more than that. In the last ten years we have witnessed the rise and dominance of the Internet. We have seen an explosion in visual literacy. Still, the art of clear written communication remains vitally important today. We hope you'll take this book in the spirit of a conversation, a lively discussion that will push forward your thinking about the writing skills that every one of our students will need.

Setting the Table for Craft

April brought a spring nor'easter. At first the ground absorbed the heavy rain. But as the rain continued to fall, surrounding lakes and streams swelled to capacity. New rivulets poured along the edges of roadways while others cut paths down wooded hillsides, creating tiny nascent waterfalls. By the time four inches had fallen the saturated landscape could hold no more. Suddenly water was washing out roadways, flooding basements, forming new lakes on people's front lawns.

By contrast, a slow and steady rain would have given the landscape time to absorb the water, ushering in luscious spring growth rather than wreaking havoc.

Students are like the earth. In today's hustle-bustle, too-much-to-teach-in-too-little-time classrooms, slow and steady may seem counterintuitive. But learning to write is a slow-growth process.

Let's say you want to teach your fifth graders to craft their stories using scenes and narration. That's a big concept, even if it is within their reach. Before students can do this deliberately and well in their own writing, they will have to:

1. Learn the language: scene, narration.

2. Understand the characteristics of scene as opposed to the quality of narration.

3. Recognize when one is best to use over the other.

This won't happen in a day. It may take weeks or months before you see the evidence in your students' writing. But don't fret. When the conditions are right, students learn. One such condition is your own sensitivity to how learning works. Teaching and learning are not consecutive acts. After you teach a lesson, you may look to your students' work and see no evidence of learning at all. But widen your view and you will likely see evidence in other, unexpected places. Maybe you have just read aloud *Owl Moon* by Jane Yolen, and a student comments, "I love the *scene* when the owl finally appears." Another student might suggest a friend write a scene at a certain part of her story. And then there may be the student who strings together one scene after another without caring in the least that the scenes don't help move the plot forward.

These examples show us learning in process (evidence of learning) as students go about reading and writing. When you teach an element of craft, you're likely to see students apply new knowledge *as readers* before they attempt to use it in their writing. Once it does make its way to their writing, you may see several missed attempts before students get it right. Such is the contour of learning. First comes awareness. Wobbly steps typically precede steady ones. As much as we'd like to believe in a magic bullet, there are no shortcuts when it comes to learning how to write.

The craft lessons in this book won't mean a hoot unless they are situated in classrooms where students are writing in authentic ways on a regular basis. Many books have been written that focus on the practicalities of running a writer's workshop. While writer's workshops will vary from classroom to classroom depending on the age of students and the personality of the teacher, you will find that all draw from a pool of shared beliefs.

Time

A soccer coach lines up her players and rolls the ball so they can trap it and shoot toward the goal. One after another, the kids score. But we need to ask: can they do it in the game? Can that girl trap the ball when it comes to her bouncing or spinning? Can that boy shoot when the ball rolls up to the right foot when he's used to shooting from the left?

Kids need to play the game. Scrimmages and actual soccer games allow young players to see the reason for particular skills ("Oh, *that's* why you need to know how to head the ball!"). In the same way, actual writing provides a rich, crucial context for students to begin to improve their writing game using specific elements of craft.

Skiers ski. They are so obsessed with skiing they will deprive themselves of all sorts of creature comforts to scrape together enough money so they can hit the slopes every chance they get. Basketball players spend countless hours practicing in gyms. The term for these creatures—gym rats—is the highest sort of compliment you can give.

Writers need to write. We tell students: a writer is somebody who writes a lot. We need to craft our daily schedules so that young writers write on a regular basis.

This book argues that direct instruction in the writer's craft has an important role in growing young writers. But it is also important that we don't overemphasize the teacher's role. Certainly there is much we can teach, but when the conditions are right, there is also much students can teach themselves and each other. In a typical writer's workshop the beginning mini-lesson is valuable, as is the ending share time, but neither will make an impact if there isn't ample time carved out for students to write.

Students need regular, sustained time to write. This means that writing has to be a planned part of the school day. When it is, the craft lessons we teach are boosted by the energy of the students' own engagement as writers. We can come up with the most brilliant craft lessons in the world. But if students write sporadically they will never have the chance to find their stride as writers.

Response

There is no greater challenge than responding to young writers who are engaged in the messy process of writing. At the same time, there is no greater joy when you approach these important interactions as they are meant to be: one-to-one conversations between a writer (the student) and a reader (you). Writers need response, not only from their peers but from us as well. The writing conference can be a place where writers are invited to think aloud about what they are attempting to do, to read their work in tandem with your more expert eyes, to see the impact their writing has on one reader. Taken together, you might say that these day-by-day conversations add up to each child's individual curriculum tailor designed to help them grow as writers.

Still, it isn't always easy. Many teachers feel so anxious about what to say in a conference that they find themselves avoiding them altogether. Don't make that mistake. Here are a few practical tips for making your writing conferences effective.

■ **Respond first as a reader.** If you want to affect the writers in your classroom, you have to let their writing affect you first. This means responding first to what it's about—content, meaning, emotional force. Laugh when the writing strikes you as funny; be puzzled if the writing confuses you. Responding in this human way earns you the right to teach a specific skill or strategy.

■ **Be positive.** Peter Elbow (1981) has remarked that a good writing teacher is both "a good host and a good bouncer." A writing teacher needs to have a positive, inviting demeanor while at the same time maintaining high standards. Early in the year you'll probably want to err on the side of being a "good host." As the year goes on, and students become comfortable with their writing, you can gradually offer more challenge.

■ **Try to understand the writer's intention.** Seek to understand what the writer is trying to do. This may require you to do a great deal of listening. When working with young writers, your listening may in fact help them name the intention that will drive their writing. What you teach in the conference will evolve from a deep understanding of the writer's intent.

■ **Help students solve their own problems.** Good writers are problem finders as well as problem solvers. When students come to you with a problem, ask them, "How might you go about fixing this?" Encourage them to try a new strategy, one they have suggested or one the two of you have thought of together.

■ **Lower your ambitions.** When we went to school we wrote infrequently, but our teachers tried to get lots of mileage out of these rare writing occasions. Students need just the reverse. They should write frequently, but we should teach no more than one or two things in each piece.

It's easy to overstay our welcome in a writing conference. When we look at a student's paper, we often see the chance to suggest several strategies, to address numerous glaring weaknesses or errors. Keep in mind that each conference is simply the next utterance in a longer conversation. Be selective about what you teach in any given moment, and know that you will build on each teaching moment in future conferences. Plus, with shorter conferences you will confer with students more frequently, which helps keep the workshop humming smoothly.

If you ask only one question in a writing conference, we suggest it be this: What are you trying to say? Everything else will flow from there. Students reread to see if they've done what they hoped to do; revisions aim to get closer to the mark. But this question only works if students take an active role in their own learning.

Responsibility

When we think back on our writing teachers, it's amazing to consider how much work they did for us. They told us what to write, how long it should be, whether or not to skip lines, whether to use cursive or printing. They told us exactly how to organize our ideas. They carefully corrected our writing and, after we handed in our final drafts, gave us a grade. We figured out what these teachers wanted, and gave it back to them. (Or not.) We were passengers on a teacher-driven mission. While these teachers surely taught us many things, they rarely taught us the process—*the inside process*—of learning to write.

Students learn more when they take responsibility for the many decisions writers face. Writers of all ages have important decisions to make. Even kindergarten writers will decide: What kind of paper should I choose? Will I begin with words or pictures? Who do I want to read this? And all writers must decide: what will I write about? Students need to feel ownership over what they write. When they don't, they'll give us blank looks when you ask: what are you trying to say?

This shifts the teacher's role. It's easy to give students a topic—harder to teach them to choose one they can write about with passion. It is quick work to mark evaluative comments on a paper—slower to teach them to assess their own words. When students are comfortable making the decisions writers face, they will grow into independent writers.

Will this happen over night? Absolutely not. As we said earlier, learning to write is a slow-growth model. But when students are making real decisions in the classroom, you can feel a heightened energy level in the room, and that energy keeps students learning.

Time, Response, Responsibility. These conditions alone won't ensure that students become skilled writers. But without regular opportunities for students to do what writers do, they will never develop the fluency necessary to make part of their repertoire the craft elements that follow. We recommend that you add two tools to these conditions—one useful, the other a necessity: the writer's notebook and literature.

The Writer's Notebook

In many classrooms students collect ideas, thoughts, artifacts, fragments of dialogue, and so forth, in a writer's notebook. There's no doubt that the writer's notebook can be a powerful tool (Fletcher 1996). Its blank pages provide a safe, no-judgment zone where students can play with language and find their strides as writers. As such, the notebook can be an ideal place for students to experiment with various elements of craft.

Imagine a fourth-grade teacher who shares "Crafting a Lead" (p. 77) with her students. At the end of this mini-lesson she might say, "We've been talking about how to write a strong lead that makes the reader want to keep reading what you have written. I invite you to try writing some leads in your writer's notebook. If you choose to do so, I'll be curious to see what leads you come up with."

Some students need to try a particular strategy themselves before it becomes part of their writing repertoire. One caution: we certainly do not want to turn the writer's notebook into a teacher-driven workbook. To the extent that the writer's notebook becomes our thing it will lose authentic power/purpose/relevance for students. Rather than *assign* we can *invite* students to use their writer's notebook as a place to "have a go" at the craft elements you have been discussing with them.

Literature

An infant born into an English-speaking home will grow up speaking English. A child born in France inevitably learns French. Likewise, students who live in a world rich with stories, songs, and poems, internalize the literate language and structures that will help them craft writing of their own. Such is the way of immersion.

The writing your students produce will be supported and sustained by the classroom literature that surrounds it. For some students, this language and literature-rich environment may be an extension of their home and earlier school lives. Others might be stepping into this world for the very first time. In either case, you will serve as their guide for living in that world with the wide-open eyes of a writer. Using literature with student writers is a huge topic; here are a few pointers.

- **Select a wide range of literature.** We've met students who love to read stories, poems, comics, or magazines. We've met others who don't read, but will sound downright encyclopedic when talking about how to catch and care for a snake. Students bring a range of passions into your classroom. Share different kinds of writing to open their eyes to the myriad ways they might write about their passions. Don't stop at books when choosing which texts to share. You'll find good writing in lots of unexpected places: newspapers, magazines, travel brochures, how-to guides, student writing folders.

- **Read aloud frequently.** If you choose only one daily ritual for your classroom, let it be reading aloud. Each time you read with students you create another common literary experience. The texts you share and the conversation that follows will help you build your community of readers and writers.

- **Reread regularly.** When our children were younger, at least 80 percent of all the reading we did with them was rereading. Our kids insisted on returning again and again to familiar, beloved books. It's clear that the more kids reread, the more things they begin to notice about the writer's craft of the text.

- **Make time for students to talk their way into an understanding of the text.** Don't underestimate the time it takes for students to develop a full and rich understanding of a text you share. This is doubly true with English language learners. Make it a habit to begin discussion with an open-ended invitation: "So, what do you think?" Be sure to invite kids to ask any questions *they* have about what they just heard. Take time to check out your students' understandings by telling back what you hear in their response: "So you think the poet is describing . . . ? What do others think?" Students need to understand what is being written before they can turn their attention to the more complicated, writerly discussion of how the author has presented the content.

- **Use specific language to talk about craft.** When the conversation shifts from the "what" (content) to the "how" (craft), avoid the tendency to use vague language. There's a world of difference between saying, "Notice how well the author describes this character" and saying, "Listen to how the author gives physical details to help us see what the character looks like." The second comment points out one specific way students can go about writing good description themselves. Students will adopt the language we use to talk about craft. At the same time we should encourage them to find their own words for speaking about craft. When a student says, "I like how the author describes," nudge the discussion to go deeper by looking together to name how the author does that.

- **Teach your students to read as writers.** When we share texts with young writers, we should ask them on a regular basis: what is something this writer is doing well? When a student comments, "I like how the author skipped around in time," we might ask her to look at how she uses time in her own story. When we help students get a feel for setting, voice, tension, inner story, or recurring detail, we are helping them develop new lenses with which to revisit their own writing. Such lenses are critical if they are going to grow into the writers they want to be.

- **Linger longer in selective texts.** We shouldn't limit our thinking when we use a book to teach a particular craft lesson. We may read a book and think, "This is a great book for teaching kids how to write better character descriptions." When you find a book you and your students love, you'll want to return to it again and again. As you reread you are likely to find a variety of potential craft lessons. *The Paperboy*, a picture book by Dav Pilkey, is written in a style that is deceptively simple. We read and reread this book and found that it could be used as a model to teach the following craft lessons:

  - Time focus—The story encompasses a narrow slice of time.

  - Repetition in language—The book uses repetition that has rhythm to it.

- Use of contrast to create tension—The story contrasts dark/light, day/night, warm/cold.

- Inner story—The story tells what the boy is thinking about.

- Point of view—The book is written in the third person. It would be a much different book if written in the first person.

- Parallel story—The boy and his dog do similar things.

- Setting—The book has a strong sense of place.

- Sensory details—The author describes using four of the five senses.

- Circular story—The book begins in the boy's bed and ends with the boy coming back to the bed, which is still warm.

- Poetic license—The book uses fragments and sentences that being with *And*.

A word of caution: Does this mean you must teach *all* these elements? NO. The list shows what students *may* learn as they come to know this book well. You'll choose which elements of craft to highlight based on the needs of your specific students. And of course, individual students may take other lessons from the text as they read as writers.

- **Use picture books for all-level learners.** Picture books offer quality writing in student-sized portions—short enough to read and reread in a time-crunched day. Their brevity can teach our students how to focus a topic appropriate for the length of writing they typically produce. Plus, a special subsection of picture books deals specifically with topics appropriate for our older readers. These books are simply too good to pass up.

Literature invites children to imagine what they themselves may one day write. It's impossible for us to envision teaching writing without it.

This chapter may seem an unnecessary obstacle to teachers eager to delve into the lessons themselves. In this regard, it's worth sharing a story about Paul, a young teacher who came to visit us in New Hampshire. When he saw all the small white pines growing around our house, his eyes grew wide.

"Would you mind if I dug up a few of those?" he asked. "I'd love to plant them around my house in Westchester, New York."

"Help yourself," we urged him. "Take as many as you want."

Paul dug up fifteen or twenty saplings, careful to preserve as much of the root ball as possible, gently packed them in his car, and drove them to his house. The next day he planted the trees.

Alas, this story does not have a happy ending. The soil at Paul's Westchester home did not agree with the white pines; all but one of them died (and even that one is struggling).

The point is a simple one. Like the pine saplings, these lessons won't successfully transplant into your classrooms unless you attend to certain essentials—time to write, careful response, student choice and responsibility, literature to model writing strategies—that will allow these craft lessons to take root and flourish in your students.

Craft Lessons K–2

atthew is ready to write. When his first-grade teacher finishes the mini-lesson, he leaves the circle at the front of the room, collects his writing folder, gathers some sheets of paper, and staples them into a book. For a few minutes he circulates around the classroom, tries to form a writing group with Brett and Lawrence, and finally decides to collaborate on a new story with Carter. He sits. Once he has found his writing partner, he fixes his attention on getting together all the materials he'll need. He has crayons, markers, and a book, but he also wants a clipboard. In fact, as he stands in front of the bookcase that holds the clipboards, he decides he needs two. Returning to his spot on the floor, he places them side by side, holds open his book, and clips one side to the left-hand clipboard, another to the right. Matthew whispers to Brett and Lawrence, who are sitting nearby and writing a cave man story.

"You're doing Cave Man Three? We'll do Cave Man Four."

"Okay," Brett replies and then adds, "We'll do all the odds, you can do the evens."

Twenty minutes ago these first graders were out running on the playground. Matthew arrived back in the classroom looking flushed, wearing catsup smears and a juice mustache from lunch. Some of his classmates flopped on the carpet, tucked fingers or a thumb into their mouths, trying to steal a moment's rest before gathering their energy for an afternoon of work.

17

In contrast, Brian has been sitting alone at a table focusing all his attention on writing about his favorite book, *The Sneetches* by Dr. Seuss. He is working diligently on his drawings of the "star on" and "star off" machines. Across the top of the paper he has written a sentence from the book in perfect copied spelling.

These beginning writers are learning to juggle the multiple demands of writing—what to write about, how to spell the words, how to organize information on paper. In many cases their choices lead them away from engaging in "writing" as we know it.

Today Elizabeth and three friends occupy the library corner in the classroom. Each are designing colorful borders on their papers. Elizabeth seems as interested in her friends' borders as in the one she is creating herself. A story might show up inside the border, but right now the artistic drive takes over and her "writing" flows from her desire to make a beautiful picture. She places a sun in the upper right-hand corner and balances the picture by placing three identical roses, one in each of the remaining three corners. Finally, she puts herself in the middle of it all holding a balloon.

We might wonder where the story is in such a piece of writing, but it is clear that more than anything Elizabeth has made a beautiful picture. First graders are particularly adept at inventing new genres, and the artistic design is a kind of writing that finds its way into the primary writing workshop.

Alexis, a second grader, is pages deep into a story about her camping trip in the mountains. There is much to tell about the three-day excursion she took with her best friend's family, and she's determined to write it all. She's already filled four pages with her large, neat handwriting—and they've just built the first campfire! Greg, a classmate, is writing a book on how to build forts. He's broken it into three parts: materials you'll need, how to get started, and step-by-step illustrated directions. Of course he can't resist also telling about the fort he and his buddies have built in his own backyard.

Donald Graves (1978) proclaimed to the world that kids can write the very first day of school. His research, based on the work he observed in Mary Ellen Giacobbi's first-grade classroom in Atkinson, New Hampshire, demonstrated that first graders can write once they know as few as eight letters. It's been twenty years since, and classrooms across the country have confirmed that first graders—and children younger—can indeed put markers to paper and engage in the work of writing.

But can these young writers *craft* their writing? Can they bring the focused deliberateness required to shape and hone a text? We believe they can, but we need to adjust our definition of *craft* and *writing* to fit the hallmark characteristics of primary-age children. Just as Graves helped us understand that drawing is writing for young children, we recognize that much of what children learn about elements of craft comes through the drawings they produce. It is often the drawings they reread, reorder, elaborate on. Young children's oral text is almost always richer than the written text they produce; similarly, much of the learning about craft takes place in the talk surrounding children's writing and drawing and may not immediately make it to the page.

At first glance, some of the lessons in this section may not look as if they are focused on teaching young writers about elements of craft. A number suggest the familiar ways you already encourage your students to simply write more—to keep the ideas flowing, to overcome the early stumbling block of wanting to spell every word correctly. We believe it is important to include such lessons because developing early fluency is such a crucial step in setting the stage for young writers to further refine their writing. Other lessons are focused on elements of craft that are within reach for beginning writers. We suggest you try to bring them to your students in the same playful, exploratory manner with which these beginning writers begin to explore the world of print.

Developing an Idea

RESOURCE MATERIAL

■ *39 Uses for a Friend* by Harriet Ziefert

ALTERNATIVE TEXTS

■ *40 Uses for a Grandpa* by Harriet Ziefert

■ *Courage* by Bernard Waber

DISCUSSION

Once young writers are comfortable choosing a topic, the next challenge may be learning to develop their ideas into something substantial and rich. This lesson invites students to spend some time brainstorming before they write.

HOW TO TEACH IT

I know a girl who is great at scoring goals in soccer. How come she's so good? Because she spends a *lot* of time shooting at the goal! Usually when someone is good at something it's because they have spent lots of time doing it. That's true for writers too. Writers are good with ideas, not just coming up with one idea, but staying with an idea for a while and really thinking about different ways to describe it fully. Harriet Ziefert does that in her book *39 Uses for a Friend*.

(Read aloud and discuss.)

To write this book, the author had to think of one use for a friend and then push her brain to come up with another and another and another until finally her book was full and interesting.

Just like Harriet Zierfert stretched her thinking to come up with a lot of ideas about a friend, you can push your brain to come up with a variety of ways to think about your big idea. Let's take the topic: a trip to the beach. If I were to write about that, I might take the idea of playing in the sand. I could tell about building a sand castle by pouring watery sand into high mounds, about burying my brother, about scratching notes with a stick, about digging a hole for my feet and letting the water pour in until I'm stuck up to my ankles. If I kept thinking, I bet I could come up with more.

Try that with one of your ideas. Before you begin writing today, take some time and think about your idea just like I thought about playing in sand. You might ask a friend to listen as you tell all the different ways you can write about your idea. Or spend time alone pushing your thinking and put as much of that thinking into your writing that you can.

Beginning, Middle, and End (1)

RESOURCE MATERIAL

■ Large chart

■ Tape, scissors, extra paper

■ Story/anecdote from your own life

ALTERNATIVE TEXTS

■ *Fireflies!* by Julie Brinckloe

■ The Magic School Bus books, by Joanna Cole, demonstrate this structure well. In each book the class prepares for the field trip, makes a journey, and returns to the classroom.

DISCUSSION

Some primary children find writing so difficult they eke out no more than a single sentence. Young children often write "attribute stories"—exploring a topic by adding one descriptive attribute: "I love my Mom." Or: "Flowers are pretty." Most children go through this stage but some seem to fixate on it, unable or unwilling to write longer, more complex stories. How do we maintain a safe, supportive environment for these writers while at the same time nudging them to wade into deeper water?

One way of extending the range of young writers is to remind them that good writing needs to have a beginning, a middle, and an end. We can introduce this idea by drawing on children's sense of story and inviting them to apply it to their own work.

HOW TO TEACH IT

(During a mini-lesson, sit in front of your students with a large chart. On the chart draw three large boxes side by side labeled BEGINNING, MIDDLE, and END.)

We have talked about how a good story has a beginning, a middle, and an end. Now I'm going to tell you a story. I want you to listen carefully. When I'm finished, I want you to tell me which part was the beginning, which part was the middle, and which part was the end.

(Tell a story from your own life. You can teach the same craft lesson by reading a picture book like *Fireflies!* by Julie Brinckloe. Then invite students to retell each part of the story, paying particular attention to beginning, middle, and end. As they do, write the parts in the appropriate boxes.)

Today I want you to think about this when you write. I want you to read over your story and ask yourself, Does my story have a beginning, a middle, and an end? If you want to add a beginning or an end to your story, you can staple another page. Or you can tape a piece of paper onto the bottom.

Beginning, Middle, and End (2)

RESOURCE MATERIAL

■ Three-page stapled blank books

DISCUSSION

Some children are fortunate enough to come from families where adults or other siblings read to them on a regular basis. These children come to school with an internalized sense of story. They know how stories work. While they can't always verbalize this understanding, their expectations guide how they listen, tell, and respond to stories.

It's common for beginning writers to tell an elaborate story that they have composed on a single sheet of paper. While their oral telling may have a sense of narrative structure, they face a huge challenge when they try to create that narrative feeling in written form. We can help students gain greater control of the narrative structure in their writing by showing them how to move from a single-sheet story to the three-page book.

HOW TO TEACH IT

Over the last few days I've listened to lots of wonderful stories. Many of you write long and involved stories, and try to fit them onto a single sheet of paper. When you share your stories with me or the class, I often hear a beginning, a middle, and an end. But when I look at your writing, the beginning, middle, and end are all mixed together on one page.

Remember that a good story has a beginning, a middle, and an end. It might help to think of your story in that way if you try writing in a book instead of on a single sheet of paper. Today on the materials table you'll notice some new books.

(Show students blank books.)

These books have three pages. Each page gives you a way to think of your story in terms of the beginning, the middle, and the end. You'll need to ask yourself, What happened first? You might write that on the first page. Then ask, What happened next? You can write that on the second page. Finally, What happened last? You might write that on the last page. If you're working on a story that has more than one part to it, choose a three-page book and see what happens.

(*Note:* Expect students to quickly grow out of the three-page book. Some will automatically want to include a cover for the title and author information. Still others will soon discover that the middle of a story usually extends beyond one page. This is true about the other parts of the story as well.)

Developing the Middle

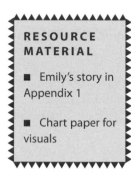

RESOURCE MATERIAL

■ Emily's story in Appendix 1

■ Chart paper for visuals

DISCUSSION

Even when young writers understand that a good story includes a beginning, a middle, and an end, they are likely to skimp on the middle. This lesson uses a metaphor and a visual to help students understand the importance of a well-developed middle.

HOW TO TEACH IT

Have you ever craved a favorite sandwich: maybe peanut butter and fluff or turkey and cheese? Now imagine. Someone hands you this sandwich, you close your eyes, mouth watering ready to take a bite and then . . . you discover there is just the thinnest film of peanut butter and hardly any fluff spread between two slices of bread. Or maybe there's only a shred of turkey and a tiny piece of cheese. You'd be pretty disappointed.

A story can be like that too. Even though there are three parts to a story—the beginning, middle, and end—readers expect that the middle will be the biggest part of the story.

Listen to this story by second grader Emily. She's written a story with a nice fat middle.

(Read aloud the untitled story by Emily.)

If you were to show this with a picture, it might look like this:

(Show design and talk about each section of the story.)

 beginning (*My Nana is everything to me. She does everything to spoil me. But that is not why I like her.*)

middle (*Point out some of the many details that make the middle.*)

end (*I love my Nana! My Nana is everything.*)

A good story usually will look like this (refer to chart you've already shown) or this,

or this, but probably not this:

If you are writing a story, ask yourself: have I given my story a nice full middle? If not, you may want to spend time beefing it up.

Match Words with the Picture

RESOURCE MATERIAL

■ *Officer Buckle and Gloria* by Peggy Rathmann

ALTERNATIVE TEXTS

■ *The Gardener* by Sarah Stewart

■ *No, David!* by David Shannon

■ *Good Boy, Fergus!* by David Shannon

DISCUSSION

In both reading and writing, we want students to appreciate that there are layers of meaning. Picture books, with illustrations and text on each page, provide a good introduction to this idea.

This is a simple but important craft lesson that builds on the "tongue-and-groove" relationship between text and illustrations. It asks students to go back, reread their stories, and check for consistency between these two symbolic worlds.

HOW TO TEACH IT

Let's revisit a book we all read and loved earlier in the year. I know you remember *Officer Buckle and Gloria.* Let's take a look at some of the pages. Do you remember how important those pictures were to the story?

You'll notice in this picture book that the pictures match the words. (Show examples from the picture book.)

If the author writes on one page about Officer Buckle watching himself on TV, you can be sure that the illustrations on that page will show the same thing. That's true about almost every picture book you read. The words and the pictures work together like a good team.

That's also true about the stories you write. A boy named Rob wrote a story that went like this: "One day I was going to the dentist." That's a perfectly good thing to write about. But when he looked underneath the words, he saw that he had drawn a picture of a dog. What's wrong with that?

(Discuss.)

When Rob noticed that his words and his picture didn't match, he wanted to fix it. He could change his story in two ways. First, he could draw a picture that went with his story. He might draw a picture of the dentist, or the dentist's building, or maybe even show some of the dentist's tools—like the drill!

Or, if he really wanted to write about the dog, he could go back and write words about the dog picture.

Whenever you write you need to ask yourself, Does my picture match my words? Do my words match my picture? It's important to check this if you're writing a story on one page. If you're writing a book with different pages, you'll want to make sure that on each page the words and the pictures work together like a good team.

Nudging Students to Move Beyond "List" and "Love" Stories

RESOURCE MATERIAL

■ *Where Are You Going, Little Mouse?* by Robert Kraus

ALTERNATIVE TEXTS

■ *Whose Mouse Are You?* by Robert Kraus

■ *The Important Book* by Margaret Wise Brown

DISCUSSION

The stories we see in primary classrooms are often sketchy. Students tell one thing about their topic, and then they're finished. One of the challenges for primary teachers is to show their students how to embellish stories and add more details. Here's how Randy Methven, a first-grade teacher in New York, describes it:

"Sometimes I realize that my kids are all writing family love stories ('I love my mother. I love my father.') and list stories ('I have a dog. My dog runs. My dog eats.'), all of which are great first writings. But I realize that the usual conference dialogue questions (What's your dog's name? What do you like to do with your mother?) aren't moving the kids beyond their simple beginnings."

HOW TO TEACH IT

Randy Methven addresses this issue in the following way:

"I begin looking for books that demonstrate answering the questions a reader might ask. A simple text like *Where Are You Going, Little Mouse?* literally demonstrates this question-and-answer process within the frame of the story:

> Whose mouse are you? Nobody's mouse.
> Where's your mother? Inside the cat . . .

"I remind the kids to think about answering in their own writing the kind of questions the mouse was asked. During writing conferences I may ask things like, Whose dog are you? Where's your boy? Asking questions like those in the story reactivates the idea of telling more and answering the readers' questions ahead of time."

Pulling a Topic from a "Grab-Bag" Piece of Writing

RESOURCE MATERIAL

■ "Me" by Mark in Appendix 2

DISCUSSION

Learning to choose a good writing topic takes time. Young children often choose to write topics close to home and end up with a loose collection of important facts that tell about themselves and their families. While this is an appropriate kind of writing for young students, we can show them how to use this kind of "grab-bag" writing as a stepping-stone to writing more focused and fleshed-out pieces.

HOW TO TEACH IT

Has anyone ever gone to a party or an event where there's a grab bag of gifts you get to choose from? It's fun. Each kid gets to reach into a bag and pull out a small wrapped present: a small sketch book, a box of markers, or maybe a little puzzle. Sometimes a piece of writing feels like a grab bag, containing many different things. Listen to this writing by Mark, a second grader.

(Read "Me.")

You learn a lot about Mark from reading his writing. He could choose any one of his sentences, open it up (just like a gift from the grab bag), and tell a whole interesting story. I bet Mark has lots to say about playing soccer and baseball. And there's probably a story he could write about himself and math. If he were to reach into this story and choose one idea to open up, maybe he would choose to tell the story about going to see a wrestling match.

Some of you may have written a "grab-bag" story just like Mark has. If you have, you can reach into that story, find one sentence, and take that idea as the topic for a brand-new piece of writing. When you do that, you'll want to take a moment to brainstorm all the things you have to say about the one idea you've chosen. This new story will be focused on one single idea and will give readers a lot more information about the idea you've chosen to focus on.

Copyright © 2007

Ralph Fletcher and

JoAnn Portalupi.

Stenhouse Publishers

Using Shared Writing to Help Students Learn to Focus

RESOURCE MATERIAL

■ Chart paper

DISCUSSION

Shared writing is an activity that builds confidence in young writers. It could be used to extend and enrich many of the lessons in this section. In this lesson, Pat Johnson, a literacy coach for the Fairfax County Public Schools, uses a shared writing experience to help students focus before they begin to write. Pat reminds us that young children need scaffolding. "It's not enough to just model and send them off. The threads of our K through 2 lessons must also be woven into some shared or community writing."

HOW TO TEACH IT

Pat suggests acting as a scribe as the children collaborate on creating a story about a common experience.

"Suppose the class just went on a field trip to a farm. The teacher would write as the children brainstorm a list of everything they did. It might look like this:

> the bus ride
> the tractor and other farm tools
> the barn
> the animals
> the hayride
> lunch in the meadow
> stopping at the park swings on the way home

"Talk with the children about how to pick one idea. You might ask: Is there one of these ideas that we could tell a lot about? Which of these ideas is most interesting to you?

"Have the children agree on an idea and proceed to write that story together. The teacher acts as scribe as the children generate their thoughts, coaching with questions as needed. What else might we add? Can we say more about that?"

Using Details (General Versus Specific)

RESOURCE MATERIAL

■ Large chart

■ Your own writing

DISCUSSION

Donald Murray (1993) points out that good writing begins with honest, specific, accurate information. In other words, believable details. That is why many teachers encourage students to begin by writing true stories based on real experiences from their own lives. Young children put in plenty of authentic details when they *tell* stories. But when they write, those details seem to disappear.

It takes a lifetime for a writer to master the effective use of details. If young writers are going to begin using details in their writing, they first need to clearly understand the difference between the general and the specific.

HOW TO TEACH IT

(Make up a large chart with two columns headed General and Specific. Under the first heading, list the general words you often see in student writing: *nice, good, fun, things.*)

I have made a list of words. These are perfectly fine words, but in a piece of writing they don't give the reader much of a picture. I might write, "My Grandpa is very nice." But when you close your eyes, it's hard to picture "nice." Right? But what if I write, "My Grandpa takes me up to the attic. He opens a big trunk and takes out his Army stuff. Sometimes he lets me wear the uniform he wore when he was a soldier." That gives you a much clearer picture, doesn't it? That's because I used details you could picture.

(Go back to the chart and list several concrete details—attic, old trunk, Army uniform—under Specific.)

Here's a challenge when you go back to your writing. Reread what you have written so far. Do you use any of these general words? Could you have used a more specific word? See if you can add some details to your story so we can picture exactly what's going on.

Using Details to Create "Mind Pictures"

RESOURCE MATERIAL

■ Your own stories

■ Students' stories

DISCUSSION

When children write their own stories, so much of the story remains in their heads that even skimpy writing can seem complete when they reread it. Lisa Siemens teaches first grade in Canada. She uses oral storytelling to show students how they can use details to create a vivid picture in the mind of the listener/reader.

HOW TO TEACH IT

"I begin by telling one of my own stories," Lisa says, "usually something from my childhood—the day a huge bee chased me all the way home as I ran barefoot down a gravelly country road. At this point there is no expectation of writing—just the simple sharing of stories. At the end of this story, I ask what pictures they saw in their minds, what they remember most. In this way I find out what details worked best. Then I ask whether anyone would like a clearer picture of anything in the story.

"'How big was the bee?' someone might ask.

"'In my mind I thought it was big as a bird, but I was not brave enough to look.'

"'How did the stones feel on your bare feet?'

"'They felt so much like pieces of glass that I thought my feet would surely be bleeding when I finally got home.'

"After my turn at telling a story, the children sign up to tell their own stories. Sometimes they have their stories thought out. Often they don't. In this case, the clarification questions serve to focus the storyteller as well as lead him to be more specific.

"Throughout the first few weeks of school, we learn about our own stories, not through writing but through telling. By the time we actually begin recording stories through drawing or writing, the children have learned not only that they have stories to tell but also that good storytelling means creating pictures or sounds or smells or feelings in people's minds. Throughout the year, I often hear them responding to other people's stories by saying, 'I'd like a better mind-picture of the part when . . .'"

Using a Comparison to Paint a Picture with Words

RESOURCE MATERIAL

■ *Owl Moon* by Jane Yolen

ALTERNATIVE TEXTS

■ "Eagle Flight," a poem by Georgia Heard

■ *The Peace Book* by Todd Parr

■ *Hello, Harvest Moon* by Ralph Fletcher

■ *Dream Weaver* by Jonathan London

DISCUSSION

We often tell students: "Add more details." But strong writing is much more than that. We don't need to wait until the upper grades to introduce students to the idea of imagery in writing. With primary writers it's probably not necessary to use terms like *simile, metaphor,* or even *imagery.* However, K through 2 students can easily pick up on the notion that writers can use comparisons to create images for the reader.

HOW TO TEACH IT

We can paint a picture using markers, crayons, colored pencils, watercolors, or paint. But writers also create a picture using words. Listen to the beginning of a poem by a boy named Matthew:

> *My mom takes good care of me.*
> *She's the gardener,*
> *I'm the rose,*
> *She waters me every day.*

Did those lines make a picture in your mind? What did you see? (Discuss.)

I don't think this writer actually means that he's a rose or that his mother truly "waters" him. He's comparing himself to a rose to describe how it feels being taken care of by his mother (the gardener).

Let's take a look at a book we know. I'm going to read one or two parts, without showing you pictures. Tell me what pictures these words make in your mind.

(Read a section from *Owl Moon*—for example, the description of the snow in the clearing.)

Do those words make pictures in your mind?

This author described something so that we could picture it in our minds. She did that by comparing the snow in a clearing to the milk in a cereal bowl.

That's my challenge for you today. See if you can use your words to create a picture for the reader. You might do this comparing one thing to another, just as these authors did.

Using Illustrations to Convey Information

RESOURCE MATERIAL

■ *A Medieval Feast* by Aliki

■ This lesson could also be done with picture storybooks published in Big Book format. We like *A Chair for My Mother* by Vera B. Williams.

ALTERNATIVE TEXTS

■ *Goodnight, Gorilla* by Peggy Rathmann

■ *Ten, Nine, Eight* by Molly Bang

DISCUSSION

Donald Graves (1983) has argued that kids can write the very first day of school. Of course, this requires us to broaden our definition of the word *writing*. For young children, drawing may serve as writing well into the early months of first grade. Rather than pushing these children into conventional print, we can learn to make use of this important time when the young writer uses drawing to compose with fluency.

Picture books offer limitless resources for focusing children's attention on the role of illustrations in telling stories. In a good picture book, the art carries meaning that is not otherwise recorded in the text.

HOW TO TEACH IT

Today we're going to read a story that you all know. But instead of reading the words, we're going to very carefully read the pictures. This will help us think about the way the pictures help to tell the story.

(Look at selected pages from *A Medieval Feast*. You might also project the illustrations onto a wall by using transparencies or an opaque projector.)

Listen to the words Aliki used to tell this part of the story.

(Quote from the text.)

Now let's look at the picture that goes with those words to see what new information the picture adds.

(Project the illustration and allow children to talk about what they are learning from the pictures. Help children notice the details the author included to present more information to her readers. Repeat with other selected pages.)

When you go back to your writing today, I'd like you to take some time to carefully read your pictures. Ask yourself if there is anything you might add that would help the reader see more of the story. Maybe you'll want to include details to better describe where your story is taking place. Or maybe you can teach us more about a character by adding details that show what that person is like.

Adding Details to Drawing

DISCUSSION

Good writing is rich in detail. For young writers the richness of their stories often resides in their imagination rather than on paper. Young writers are often content to represent the whole of a story with the most minimal sketch. But even the youngest writer can be taught to reread and elaborate a story when we shift the focus from the writing to the drawing. The child who is practiced at looking at her drawing and asking, Have I added enough detail? is well on her way to developing skill at the critical reading and revision we will ask her to do later in her writing.

HOW TO TEACH IT

(While this might easily be used as a whole-class lesson, you could also use it during individual conferences with children who use drawing to represent specific events or stories. Begin by asking the child to talk about what is happening in the story. Through active listening, encourage the child to explain the details of the story. Respond by telling back some of what you heard. Then ask the child to look with you at the written version—the drawing—to see where certain details are represented.)

Raymond, you're writing about your trip to the dentist. How will a reader know from looking at this picture that you were at the dentist? What could you include that would help the reader feel like he or she was there?

(Use the information that the child shares to direct your questioning. When the conference is complete, take a minute to reflect on the rereading strategy you taught.)

Before I leave let's think about what you did today. First, I asked you to tell your story in order to help you think about the details that are an important part of it.

You then looked carefully at your drawing to see if you had included enough details on the paper. When you did that, you discovered there were some things you left out. Adding them to your drawing helped make your writing stronger. Each time you write, you'll want to ask yourself this important question: Have I included enough detail to help a reader understand the story?

(If you want to teach this element of craft in a mini-lesson, invite a child to coteach it with you. Do this by having a public conference on the above strategy or by re-creating the conference, and show the class the way the writer added details to the drawing.)

Use Your Voice When You Write

RESOURCE
MATERIAL

■ *I'll Fix Anthony*
by Judith Viorst

ALTERNATIVE
TEXTS

■ *The Hello,
Goodbye Window*
by Norton Juster

■ *My Little
Brother* by David
McPhail

■ *My Five Senses*
by Aliki

DISCUSSION

Let's face it: even the idea of writing scares some kids to death. Faced with pencils, tiny symbols, impossible-to-spell words, many children simply freeze up. Writing teachers know that *risk-taking* and *fluency* form the bedrock of a strong writer's workshop, particularly for children at this age. It's important to do whatever you can to make writing seem less threatening and more manageable.

This craft lesson builds on the natural link between spoken and written language. It gives primary children an introduction to the idea of voice in writing.

While children tend to use the "I" in their writing, most picture books for kids of this age are written in the third person. Books written in the first person provide strong models for kids to use their own voices. We suggest four such books, but you might have other favorite texts written in the first person that your children are already familiar with. If so, you can use those.

HOW TO TEACH IT

Imagine that you just had a sleepover with a really good friend. You are sitting at the kitchen table, talking to your friend.

Well, that's what writing is. Think of writing as chatting on paper. You use your voice but instead of speaking out loud you let your voice speak on the paper. You talk to the reader when you write down words.

Most of you know *I'll Fix Anthony*. I'm going to read a few pages from this book. Listen carefully because I want you to notice how it sounds as if the author is talking to us. You can hear her speaking.

(Read a few pages. Discuss.)

You can do the same thing that Judith Viorst did in her book. Today when you write you can try to make your words sound just the way you sound when you talk to a friend. Let's say that I talk like this:

"I always forget something important when I go to the store. Well, last Saturday I came home with ten bags of groceries and—disaster! Wouldn't you know it? I forgot the cake mix for my son's birthday party!"

When I write about this, I can write the same words that I just said to you.

(You might model this by writing it down on a big chart.)

Try to use your talking voice today when you're writing words. You might even want to talk softly out loud as you're writing down the words.

How to Pace a Story

RESOURCE
MATERIAL

■ Three- or four-page stapled blank books

■ *Little Nino's Pizzeria* by Karen Barbour

■ *Goose* by Molly Bang

ALTERNATIVE
TEXTS

■ *Good Boy, Fergus!* by David Shannon

■ *Kitten's First Full Moon* by Kevin Henkes

DISCUSSION

Primary writing teachers work hard so their students can get into a groove and find a nice writing flow. We try hard to defuse issues of spelling, saying, "When in doubt, sound it out!" or simply, "Guess and go."

But at the same time we often need to slow these writers down. Otherwise they tell everything on the very first page. It's helpful for young writers to see ways that they can slow down their stories, to reveal the story bit by bit instead of blurting it all out at one time.

HOW TO TEACH IT

I could write, "My father came to visit and repaired ten broken things the very first day! I told him he can come to visit whenever he wants!"

But if I write it that way, I'm telling the whole story on the very first page. My story might sound better if I slowed it down and stretched it out over several pages. On the first page I could write about how he fixed the doorbell. On the second page, I could write about how he fixed the dripping faucet.

Let's look at a book you all know, *Little Nino's Pizzeria*. I'm going to read it again. I want you to notice how Karen Barbour tells a little bit of the story on each page.

(Read. Discuss.)

I want you to notice something about this book. Sometimes this author writes one sentence on a page. But sometimes she takes one sentence and stretches it out over several pages.

(Show.)

The same thing happens with *Goose*. Look at how the first part of this sentence—"On a dreadfully dark and stormy night"—goes on the first page. And then the second part of the sentence—"an egg was blown right out of its nest"—goes on the second page.

I want you to think about this today when you write. You don't have to jam your whole story into the very first page. You can slow down, spread out. Think about feeding your story to the reader bit by bit. I've made up some blank books if you want to use them in your writing.

Writing a Strong Lead

DISCUSSION

Trying out various leads for a piece of writing would seem like a strategy perhaps more suited to upper-grade students. But teachers can help even emerging writers become aware of how a lead can strengthen a piece of writing. Here Lisa Siemens, a primary teacher in Canada, explains how she teaches it.

HOW TO TEACH IT

"I print out several particularly strong leads on paper cut in the shape of an arrow. I make sure to use leads written by professionally published writers as well as writers from the class. I try to pick books that they already know and love, as well as leads written in the first, second, or third person. Many of the children are writing in the first person, yet most of the literature they read tends to be written the third person.

"I hold the arrows up one at a time, explaining that the first line in a story is often the line that makes the reader decide whether he or she is interested in a particular book. Then I tell them that the first line or two is called the lead.

"'What does lead mean?' I ask. Usually someone says it is something you want to follow. 'Exactly,' I respond. 'A good lead makes you want to follow it. When you read a good lead, you know it. When you write a good lead you know it.'

"When I send them off to write, I simply ask that they read their lead to themselves and see whether it leads them on. We post our arrows on our classroom door, and they become invitations to enter our classroom, invitations to literature. Then, as the days pass, we print out other strong leads we notice in either our writing or our reading."

Writing a Strong Ending

RESOURCE MATERIAL

■ *If You Give a Mouse a Cookie* by Laura Numeroff

■ *No, David!* by David Shannon

ALTERNATIVE TEXTS

■ *Koala Lou* by Mem Fox

■ *Owl Babies* by Martin Waddell

DISCUSSION

We need to constantly "fill the storehouses" of our young writers. The purpose of these craft lessons is to offer students many ways to craft and revise their writing. Eventually they will have a repertoire of options and strategies available to them. This lesson aims to develop students' story sense in terms of the ending.

HOW TO TEACH IT

Every story should have a beginning, a middle, and an end. We have talked about the beginning and the middle. Today let's talk about the end. What makes a good ending in a story?

(Discuss. You may want to jot down students' responses.)

Your ending is important—it's the last thing the reader will read. You can't just write THE END and be done with it! You want to write a strong ending. Jackson, a first grader, wrote a story that went like this:

Mom says I broke my shoulder when I was born.
After that I broke my ankle.
One time I broke my pinky finger.
Another time I cracked a rib.
I broke a tooth playing baseball.
What bone I will break next?

Jackson ended his story with a question. That's one way you could end your story. Let's take a look at some books we have read, and see how these authors ended their stories.

In *No, David!* everyone tells David, No! But on the second-to-last page, the story changes. And on the last page David finally hears: Yes, David. What kind of ending would you call that?

(Discuss. Kids may call it a happy ending.)

If You Give a Mouse a Cookie starts with this sentence: "If you give a mouse a cookie. . . ." This book has a beginning and an ending that are almost the same. It makes a circle. Like a circle, it starts all over again.

Today when you write, think about your ending. You could end with a question. You could end with a circular ending, a happy ending, even a sad ending. Or maybe you'll come up with your special ending. See if you can write an ending that is just as good as the rest of your story.

Surprise Endings

RESOURCE MATERIAL

■ *Just Like Daddy* by Frank Asch

ALTERNATIVE TEXTS

■ *No, David!* by David Shannon

■ *Guess What?* by Mem Fox

DISCUSSION

Probably the simplest kind of surprise ending is one that relies on the structure of the story to set up the surprise. Young children can begin to experiment with this kind of surprise ending and, at the same time, start to think about patterns in stories. Of course, the challenge is in the careful selection of the surprising detail. As young writers begin to experiment with patterns in stories, they will learn to refine them in order to elicit the reader's laughter.

HOW TO TEACH IT

Today I want to talk about surprise endings. I want to show you a way a writer can set the reader up for a surprise at the very end. Lots of times a story follows a very simple pattern. When the writer follows a very clear pattern you begin to think you know what is coming next. Just when you think you know what is coming . . . Surprise! The writer gets you by breaking the pattern.

(Read *Just Like Daddy*.)

Could you hear the pattern in Frank Asch's story? He made it by repeating the same line over and over again. By the time we get to the end of the story, we're convinced that this story is about a father and his child. We forget all about the mother until she shows up on the last page.

To make this kind of a surprise ending you'll need to have a strong pattern in your story. Is there an important line that can repeat until the last page? If there isn't a line, maybe there is an event that occurs over and over again that might change on the last page. Try experimenting with different ways to make a pattern. Once the pattern is in place you can surprise your readers by changing it at the very end.

Copyright © 2007

Ralph Fletcher and

JoAnn Portalupi.

Stenhouse Publishers

Fleshing Out Sketchy Writing by Cutting and Pasting

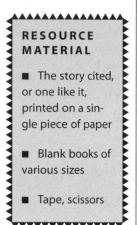

RESOURCE MATERIAL

■ The story cited, or one like it, printed on a single piece of paper

■ Blank books of various sizes

■ Tape, scissors

DISCUSSION

We can show young writers how to manipulate the texts they are working on. While this may not immediately lead to great results, it's important for kids to understand at an early age that their stories aren't etched in stone, that they can be playful when they write. If a craft lesson like this one is going to affect young writers, the teacher needs to demonstrate the strategy using tape, paper, scissors. You'll find that your students pay close attention when you do so.

HOW TO TEACH IT

You may read over something you wrote and say to yourself, "Hey, I think I want to add more. There are some things I've left out." Let me show you one way you can do that. Here's a story that Emily wrote when she was in first grade:

My Grammy lives on a farm.
She lives in Israel.
Right now she is very sick.
Everybody is worried.
I hope she's going to be okay.

Imagine this is your story. Let me show you something you could do with it. Watch this.
(Demonstrate.)
You could cut out this first sentence—"My Grammy lives on a farm"—and tape it to a blank page in this book. You might tape it up here. Maybe there are goats on Grammy's farm. Maybe she grows olives on the farm. Well, now you've got all this room to write about that. And you can make a picture to go with what you write.
You could do this with the next sentence—"She lives in Israel." You could cut out that part and tape it to the next blank page. Now, you've got room to add more about Israel. You could write more or draw a map of Israel. You could do it with your whole story. This is a great way to stretch out your story and add more details.
I've made some blank books for anyone who would like to try this. We've got tape and scissors right here in the writing center. Go to it.

Time Transitions

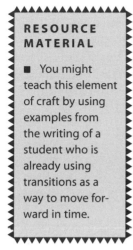

DISCUSSION

Second or third graders are notorious for the "bed-to-bed" story, in which the writing closely mirrors the events of real life. It will take years before young writers are able to deliberately shape a story in effective fashion, but they can start this process now. We can help students learn to manipulate time by pointing out the language writers use to move from one point in time to another. There really is a way to get from breakfast to dinner without having to stop for lunch!

HOW TO TEACH IT

When you write, you don't have to include everything that happened between one time and another. For instance, let's say you are writing about spending the weekend at your cousin's house. You want the story to start when you burst into your house after school that Friday all excited to go. And let's say you want the story to end when you arrive home Sunday night. You wouldn't have to tell every little thing that happened in between. You would probably want to tell certain parts of the weekend, but there would be some places you would want to skip over. Today I want to share with you some of the words or phrases writers use to help them jump forward in time.

(Generate a list similar to the following. Provide examples as needed.)

> The next day . . .
> Later that night (or afternoon) . . .
> Later in the day . . .
> In the morning . . .
> After awhile . . .
> Finally . . .
> Next . . .

These words allow you to skip ahead in time and leave things out of your writing that aren't important.

Before you begin writing today, I'd like you to read what you've already written. See if you've included some events that you'd prefer to leave out. If so, you may want to use one of these words or phrases to skip forward in time. You may come up with another word that lets you skip forward. If you do, make sure to add it to our list.

Using "Talk Bubbles"

RESOURCE MATERIAL

■ Large chart

ALTERNATIVE TEXTS

■ *Mama* by Jeannette Winter

■ The Magic School Bus series by Joanna Cole

■ *The Popcorn Book* by Tomie de Paola

DISCUSSION

Primary-age students typically talk a great deal. But the characters in their stories rarely do any talking. This is understandable. Using dialogue is a stretch for most young writers, and the challenge of using quotation marks makes the task seem insurmountable. Here is an easy way you can introduce dialogue to primary writers without getting bogged down in all the particulars of quotation marks.

HOW TO TEACH IT

(Make sure your students are familiar with a picture book that uses "talk bubbles" to indicate spoken dialogue. You could use *The Popcorn Book* or any of The Magic School Bus books.)

Did you notice that in this book the characters did a lot of talking to each other? Let's take a look at how the author showed us that they were talking. Look at this illustration on this page. Do you see those big things coming out of the characters' mouths? Those are called talk bubbles or talk balloons. You can see that they each point to a character. If you read what is inside the talk bubble, you can see what that character is saying.

You can do this in your writing. Maybe there has been a time when you were writing a story and you wanted to have some of your characters talk. Talk bubbles give you an easy way to do it.

(You might illustrate the following on a large chart.)

Let's say I want to write a story about a boy telling his father that he has lost a tooth. First, I'll have to make a picture of both characters.

(Draw.)

Then I'll draw a bubble above or beside each picture and write the spoken words inside each bubble. My readers will know that the words inside these bubbles are spoken words coming out of the character's mouth.

I'll be interested in seeing if any of you try this idea in your own writing.

New Ways to Write About an Old Topic

RESOURCE MATERIAL

■ Large chart

■ *Fireflies!* by Julie Brinckloe

■ *Fireflies in the Night* by Judy Hawes

■ "Firefly" by Elizabeth Madox Roberts (see Appendix 3)

DISCUSSION

A few years ago one first-grade teacher told her students, "I'm sorry, but I just can't read another story about Ninja Turtles. No more stories about Ninja Turtles. Today I'm going to ask you to choose something different to write about." One boy raised his hand and sweetly asked, "Like what?"

Donald Graves says that we need to encourage writers to bring their obsessions into the writing workshop. Well, young writers certainly do that. But many get so stuck on a topic—cats, weapons, race cars—they seem incapable of writing about anything else. This craft lesson shows young writers new ways of exploring the subjects they are passionate about.

HOW TO TEACH IT

These authors each wrote about fireflies, but they wrote about this subject in different ways. This one, *Fireflies!* by Julie Brinckloe, tells a story. It has a beginning (when he sees the fireflies flashing), a middle (when he catches them), and an end (when he decides to let them go). (Share.)

This one, *Fireflies in the Night*, is an information book. In this book the author teaches us about fireflies. It taught me lots of things about fireflies that I didn't know before. (Share.)

Elizabeth Madox Roberts wrote a *song* about fireflies. (Share Appendix 3.)

So there you have it. The same topic, fireflies, written three different ways. And you could do the same thing. I've noticed that many of you often choose to write about the same topic. Let's say you like to write about horses. Here are some ways you could write about this topic. (Show on chart.)

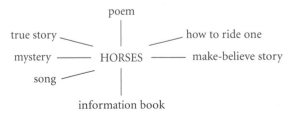

I'll be curious to see if today you find a new way to write about the topics you like to write about.

Describing the Setting

▀ **RESOURCE MATERIAL**

■ Your original writing with illustrations

■ *The Paperboy* by Dav Pilkey

■ *Tar Beach* by Faith Ringgold

■ *Up North at the Cabin* by Marsha Wilson Chall

DISCUSSION

All stories have a setting. In the rush to highlight people or events, beginning writers often pay little attention to where their stories take place. Yet the setting is perhaps one of the easiest elements of craft they can attend to simply by detailing it in their drawings.

HOW TO TEACH IT

(Gather a few well-loved picture storybooks that take place in a variety of settings. For this lesson we pull together *The Paperboy*, *Up North at the Cabin*, and *Tar Beach*.)

Today we're going to look at some books we already know, but we're going to read them differently than we usually do. I'm going to ask each of you to be very quiet as I turn the pages. Look carefully at the pictures of each story. I want you to pay attention to where the story is taking place. When we're done, we'll talk about what we saw.

(Hold up the books and page through the pictures. You may occasionally add a little summary as needed to keep students engaged.)

Each of these stories takes place in a different setting. Let's list the different places: small-town neighborhood, lake, city.

(Continue with a discussion of how illustrators include information to fully develop the sense of place. Next, hold up a piece of writing with pictures that typify the lack of detail young writers give to the settings of their stories. We suggest you generate an original piece rather than drawing negative attention to an individual student's writing.)

Let's read this story in the same way. See if you can tell where this story takes place.

(Look at the illustrations as you did with the published books. Discuss ways the author could enrich the setting in her illustrations.)

When you return to your writing today, take a minute to think about where your story takes place. Could a reader tell from looking at your drawings? If not, is there something you can add to the pictures or to the words that will help?

Copyright © 2007

Ralph Fletcher and

JoAnn Portalupi.

Stenhouse Publishers

Using Details to Describe the Setting

RESOURCE MATERIAL

■ *My Little Island* by Frane Lessac

ALTERNATIVE TEXTS

■ *The Hello, Goodbye Window* by Norton Juster

■ *Shortcut* by Donald Crews

DISCUSSION

Young children often draw the main elements of their stories without situating them in a larger context. Maria writes a story about losing a tooth and draws a frontal picture of herself smiling to reveal the new gap in her teeth. She tells us she was in music class when her tooth fell out, but we can't see that from the words or the illustration. In fact, she's floating in the middle of the page—the main character in an otherwise empty landscape.

It's common for a beginning writer like Maria to ignore the setting of her story. It may be years before she develops the skill to integrate information about setting into her text. But it's not too early for her to learn about this necessary element of writing. In a good picture book, illustrations do much of the work of establishing the setting of the story. We can begin talking with young children about setting by observing the way illustrators include this information in their artwork.

HOW TO TEACH IT

Every story takes place somewhere. Some of you are writing stories that take place at your house or here at school. Others are writing stories that take place in faraway settings like the beach or the mountains. No matter where a story takes place, writers like to help readers feel like they are there. Writers do this by including information about place in the words and also in the pictures. Today we're going to read a story and then think about what the author/illustrator does to help us learn about where her story takes place.

(Read *My Little Island*. Make sure students are gathered close enough to see the pictures. You may want to project the illustrations using an opaque projector or color transparencies. In discussion, talk about the many details included in the drawings that help describe the setting of the island. Note how Lessac uses color and detailed illustrations to show the homes and clothing of the people as well as the various plants that grow there.)

When you go back to your writing today, I'd like you to think about the setting of your story. Take some time to look carefully at your pictures. Ask yourself if there is anything you might add to help the reader learn about where the story is taking place.

Focus: Staying on the Topic

▲▲▲▲▲▲▲▲▲▲▲▲

RESOURCE MATERIAL

■ "Changing a Tire," story excerpt (see Appendix 4)

▼▼▼▼▼▼▼▼▼▼▼▼

DISCUSSION

Have you ever seen a group of young children play softball or whiffle-ball? At first the game may bear some resemblance to how adults play the game. But suddenly a dog snatches the ball and the children start chasing it across the yard. The softball game fluidly flows into chase-the-dog.

This is similar to the way primary children write. Kids at this age are notoriously unfaithful to their subjects. How many times have we seen a child begin describing something and suddenly, with no warn-ing, start writing about something completely new? This is the nature of writers at this age, but we can begin making them aware of focus and its importance.

HOW TO TEACH IT

Sometimes we start writing but we wander off the topic. Often we're writing along and don't even realize that this happened. When you go back and reread what you've written, you can find out whether or not you stayed on the topic.

I'm going to read you a little story. I think you'll find a few places where this author wandered off the topic and started writing about something that has nothing to do with what the story is really about. After I read this we can talk about it.

(Read "Changing a Tire" and discuss. You might put the story on a large chart or overhead.)

Where are the places where this author got off the topic? I'm going to cross out these parts.

This is one of the most important writer's questions you can ask yourself: Did I stay on this topic? I want you to pay attention to this, especially if you have finished your piece of writing. The only way to know for sure is to go back and reread what you've written. You might even want to read it to a friend. Then you can both listen. If you find parts where you got off the topic, you can cross them out just like we did today.

Cause and Effect

RESOURCE MATERIAL

■ *Lilly's Purple Plastic Purse* by Kevin Henkes

ALTERNATIVE TEXTS

■ *A Good Day* by Kevin Henkes

■ *Old Henry* by Joan W. Blos

Copyright © 2007

Ralph Fletcher and

JoAnn Portalupi.

Stenhouse Publishers

DISCUSSION

There's a wonderful spontaneity about primary-grade writing. Writers at this age rarely do much planning, happy to make it up as they go along. As a result, their writing often has a carefree, almost random feel to it. Monsters appear out of nowhere, then vanish. A story begins one way, turns, and bolts in a completely different direction. Teachers who work with primary writers learn to make peace with this developmental stage. But at the same time we can make young writers aware of certain expectations—sense, plausibility, sequence—that readers bring to a piece of writing.

Cause and effect falls into this category. This is another way to help students flesh out skeletal writing by sketching in the connections between events.

HOW TO TEACH IT

Most things happen for a reason. In other words, one thing causes another. If you throw a rock into a beehive, that will probably cause the bees to get angry and start swarming out. And there's a good chance that might cause you to get stung. The three things are connected:

A ———→ B ———→ C

It's no different in the books we read. If something happens in a book, it usually causes something else to happen. Remember *Lilly's Purple Plastic Purse*? Lilly loves her teacher until Mr. Slinger takes away her purple plastic purse. When he does that, she gets really mad. Now that she's mad, she goes home and writes a mean note about her teacher. The next day she gives it to him. You know what happens next.

Lots of events are connected by cause and effect. Today when you write I want you to think about this. If something happens in your story, think about what caused it to happen. Maybe your little brother was acting extra-hyper one day and he knocked over a lamp and broke it. What caused him to act extra-hyper? Maybe it was the day after Halloween and he had eaten too much candy!

If something happens in your story, you need to ask yourself, Will this cause something else to happen later in my story?

Physical Description of a Character

RESOURCE MATERIAL

■ *Henry and Mudge and the Happy Cat* by Cynthia Rylant

■ Chart containing printed description of the cat

■ Sticky notes

ALTERNATIVE TEXT

■ *The Ticky-Tacky Doll* by Cynthia Rylant

DISCUSSION

Bringing characters alive is hard for writers of every age. Perhaps the easiest way for young writers to begin developing the characters in their writing is to attend to the physical traits of those characters. Because physical characteristics are external, students can act as reporters by writing down what they see when they visualize a character in their mind's eye.

HOW TO TEACH IT

When we think back on a story, it's often the characters that we remember most. This happens because the writer has made them seem real in our minds. One way a writer does this is by providing details that help us picture what the character looks like. Listen to the description Cynthia Rylant uses in her book *Henry and Mudge and the Happy Cat.*

> It had a saggy belly,
> skinny legs,
> and fur that looked like
> mashed prunes.

Cynthia Rylant describes what she sees when she looks at the newly found cat. These few physical details she gives help us to make a picture of the cat in our minds.

Many of you have stories with one or more characters in them. Do you have a character you could describe in this way to help us picture him or her?

(Invite students to imagine the character in their mind's eye and to talk aloud about what they see. You might record some of the language on a sticky note and give it to them to have when they return to their writing.)

Revealing the Inside Story

RESOURCE MATERIAL

■ "First Day of School" by Zhou

■ Two different-colored markers

DISCUSSION

Many primary children find writing to be a daunting task. They are often content to do no more than jot a brief summary or synopsis of what happened. This lesson encourages them to deepen their writing by revealing the interior life of the narrator.

HOW TO TEACH IT

When you write a story, you can do more than just tell what happened *to* you. You can also tell what happened *inside* you: what you were thinking, how you were feeling. Let's take a look at a story by a first-grade writer. Zhou goes to school in New York City. Here's the story he wrote:

> One early sunny morning I went to school. It was the first day of school. I was very excited and little bit scared. My teacher is Ms. Yung and Ms. Sanchez. I was happy.
>
> But I did not know who will be my friend. I was nervous—I went in the class and I saw Ryan. I was excited.
>
> I play logo with Ryan. We built a car. In the end of school I was not scared. I have a friend. My good friend is Ryan.

The "outside story" is what happened in the story—the plot. What might that include in Zhou's story?

(As students respond, underline the sentences that tell the outside story with one colored marker.)

■ First day of school.
■ His teacher is Ms. Yung and Ms. Sanchez.
■ He played logo at school.

How about the "inside story"? What was Zhou thinking and feeling?

(Underline students' responses [the inside story] with a different-colored marker.)

■ He felt excited and a little bit scared.
■ He felt nervous in class.

Including the inside story will make your writing richer and more interesting. Today as you write, see if you can include the inside story.

Writing Through a Mask

▲▲▲▲▲▲▲▲▲▲▲▲▲

RESOURCE MATERIAL

■ *I Stink!* by Kate and Jim McMullan

ALTERNATIVE TEXTS

■ *I'm Dirty!* by Kate and Jim McMullan

■ *Sierra* by Diane Siebert

▼▼▼▼▼▼▼▼▼▼▼▼▼

DISCUSSION

Young writers are no different from the rest of us. At times their writing falls into a rut, and we find ourselves looking for a spark to liven it up.

Writing through a mask (personification is the fancy word for it) is one way of helping students to jazz up tired writing and stretch the language in their writing. This strategy builds on young children's love of pretend and games of the imagination.

HOW TO TEACH IT

When Robert was a little boy, he loved to pretend. Every day he woke up pretending he was a different animal. Some days he was a baby seal. Other days he was a rattlesnake, or a turtle who couldn't find his mother. Some mornings we had to take care of this new animal in our house and feed it a special breakfast.

Maybe you like to pretend like Robert. Lots of authors do. I'm going to read you a book where the authors pretend they are a garbage truck. Can you image what it would be like to be a garbage truck? Let's see how the authors wrote it.

(Read *I Stink!*)

Today you might decide to try what Kate and Jim McMullan do in this book. When you write, you might pretend you're a bike, or the wind, or a tree in your neighborhood. A first-grade writer wanted to describe what it would be like to be the grass. Here's how she described it:

I am the gras	I am the grass
the cids owys STOMP on me	the kids always STOMP on me
I hate that!!!!!	I hate that!!!!!

Think of trying this in your writing. Maybe you'll pretend you're the moon. What would it feel like to be the moon? What would you say? How could you describe it?

Craft Lessons: Teaching Writing K–8 **SECOND EDITION**

Trying a Back-and-Forth Pattern

RESOURCE MATERIAL

■ *Fred Stays with Me!* by Nancy Coffelt

ALTERNATIVE TEXTS

■ *The Difference Between Babies and Cookies* by Mary Hanson

■ *My Mom Travels a Lot* by Caroline Feller Bauer (A perfect book for introducing patterned writing—out of print, but may be available.)

DISCUSSION

One of the ways that readers achieve a sense of satisfaction from a story comes from the way the story is designed. A well-designed story has order and logic to it. Even the youngest children can begin experimenting with story structure in their own writing by imitating simple patterned texts.

HOW TO TEACH IT

Every story has a shape to it. One way to shape a story is by making a back-and-forth pattern. In this kind of pattern the story bounces back and forth between two or more ideas.

(Read *Fred Stays with Me!*)

Do you hear the pattern? Nancy Coffelt makes a pattern by alternating between her mom, her dad, and Fred, her dog. A story like this often ends with the pattern breaking or, as in this case, with the ending circling back to the beginning.

(Reread the beginning and ending of *Fred Stays with Me!*)

Sometimes the topic we want to write about might fit into a back-and-forth pattern. Let's say you want to compare two or three different things. You might start by brainstorming a list of details for each idea. Then see if you can put them into a pattern by alternating details from your lists.

You'll also want to think about the very end. Do you want to end by breaking the pattern? Or will you end by repeating the opening sentence, like Coffelt did?

Repeating a Word

RESOURCE MATERIAL

■ Song and child's poem cited

■ "Things," poem by Eloise Greenfield from *Honey, I Love*

ALTERNATIVE TEXTS

■ *Suddenly!* by Colin McNaughton

■ *Terrific* by Jon Agee

DISCUSSION

Repetition is a simple technique primary children can use to bring music to their writing. This craft lesson draws on a familiar song, a child's poem, and a book that can be read quickly to illustrate the point.

HOW TO TEACH IT

Sometimes an author will take one word or one part and say it more than once. That's called repetition. The parts that get repeated really stick in your mind. You can hear it in songs you know by heart:

> Row, row, row your boat
> Gently down the stream,
> Merrily, merrily, merrily, merrily,
> Life is but a dream.

Did you hear the words that got repeated? Melanie, a first-grade writer, decided to do the same thing in this poem she wrote. She repeated the first word of the poem:

> Turtle, turtle,
> You look so little,
> You walk so slow,
> You look like an
> upside-down soup bowl!

The part that gets repeated acts like the glue that holds the writing together. You remember this poem "Things" by Eloise Greenfield. She repeats the last line of each stanza.

Repetition is something you can try in your own writing. You can take a favorite word or line and repeat it as many times as you like. I'll be very curious to see if any of the writers here try this idea.

The Repeating Line

RESOURCE MATERIAL

■ *The Doorbell Rang* by Pat Hutchins

■ "My Dog" (see Appendix 5)

ALTERNATIVE TEXTS

■ *Bee-bim Bop!* by Linda Sue Park

■ *King Bidgood's in the Bathtub* by Audrey Wood

■ *We Share Everything* by Robert Munsch

■ *Mothers Are Like That* by Carol Carrick

■ *Titch* by Pat Hutchins

DISCUSSION

The previous craft lessons show a way to invite children to try out variations of pattern writing. Some books, however, ask the reader to dig deeper to find out the pattern being used.

Take the repeating line. We have already talked about repeating words, but some writers will take a sentence and bring it back again and again in a story or poem. A repeating line can bring cohesion to the writing. And it can build emotional power as it gets repeated in the text. Repetition is a strategy well within the reach of many primary-grade writers.

HOW TO TEACH IT

We've been talking about the different kinds of patterns that writers use in their books and poems. You're getting good at noticing patterns and figuring them out. Let's try another one. You may have read these books before; now try to figure out the pattern.

(Read *The Doorbell Rang*.)

Some of you noticed that the author took this line—"and the doorbell rang"—and repeated it throughout the book.

Here's a poem by a second grader. This writer also uses a line that repeats.

(Read "My Dog.")

I wonder if any of you would like to try a pattern like this. Here's how you might do it. As you write, decide on a sentence you would like to repeat. It could be a funny part, it could be an important part, it could just be your favorite part. As you write your story, you can repeat that part as many times as you want. As you're doing that, decide whether or not you'd like to change your pattern at the very end.

Craft Lessons 3–4

*I*n Carolyn Lytle's third-grade classroom, Claire and Amy sit together on the carpet. Their writer's notebooks lay scattered on the floor in front of them, along with a collection of trade books about well-known people who have battled personal or political hardships in their lives.

"We're writing strong poems," Claire explains. "Poems about people who have been treated wrong."

Claire opens her notebook and gives a short history of the project.

"We began with Acrostics, but we decided we wanted to write something stronger."

If you listen to the seriousness and ambitious intentions of these girls, you might mistake them for much older students. But look at their work and you see the characteristic hallmarks of the nine-year-old. Third graders can write faster than their younger peers, but their letters are often still large and rounded, and their pace of writing can be slowed by the drawing of letters.

The two girls have written five poems so far—"Rosa Parks," "Ruby Bridges," "Trail of Tears," "A Power of Heart" (a poem about cruelty toward blacks), and "The Luckiest Man" (about Lou Gehrig). The poems range from six to ten lines each, and look to be mostly in first-draft form. It's clear that these students are more focused on generating enough "strong poems" than on carefully rereading or revising any of the individual poems.

In another third-grade class the kids are writing quietly. One boy leans over to a friend and points at the teacher.

"Put in lots of feelings," he whispers. "She loves feelings."

Many third graders strive to please their teachers. For many students, the next two years will be a time of gradually turning their attention away from seeking adult approval toward seeking approval from their peers. As this redefined social awareness finds its way into the classroom, writing workshop becomes infused with a new and intense kind of social play. Peers become an increasingly important audience for students at this age. While Amy and Claire have focused their attention on oppression in the outside world, their joint project gives them a way of defining and developing the relationship between them. Students at this age like to name each other as characters in their fictional stories. Granting permission for the use of your name in a story is a kind of social capital that allows students to invest in relationships with peers.

For third and fourth graders, the social nature of writing readily contributes to their developing knowledge of craft. As students collaborate on writing projects, they engage in focused and sustained conversations about their writing. These relationships require that students plan the process of their work; they also provide a context for talking about craft itself.

Primary writers tend to see their writing as an extension of themselves: if it makes sense to me, it's okay. By third and fourth grade, students have a greater need to make their writing work for others. They will listen to comments and suggestions offered by peers and, with encouragement and support, incorporate these responses into their writing. (Sometimes.)

Concrete strategies for making changes are still the most likely route to revision (taping a paper flap, using a code, crossing out). But by late in fourth grade, more mature writers can begin to outgrow these techniques and opt for the true second draft. Now the student can write a new draft of a story where substantive changes in content or form have taken place.

Caley writes a story about a vacant house and a family who moves in. Soon the neighbors notice two new girls spying in the bushes. By the end of the story the girls are taking a trip with their new neighbors to Disney World. It's clear that the pleasure of writing comes in the topic—a fantasy Caley would like to have herself.

"I wanted to make it a mystery, but I couldn't," Caley says during share time. These students have a growing awareness of different kinds of writing, even if they aren't proficient in all of them. The fact that Caley can name this new genre will pave the way for learning how to create it.

With their new fluency and confidence, third and fourth graders can grapple with a whole new set of writing skills. They can learn about focusing a topic, giving weight to significant information, developing characters, and writing strong leads and more appropriate endings. They can use their newfound knowledge of genre to sharpen their intentions. Now, along with choosing a topic, they can decide how to write about that topic. A summer camp experience might yield a personal narrative, a poem, or even a guide to surviving summer camp. These students understand the need to write from information; their work is enriched by the research they do on their topics.

Tools (dictionary, thesaurus, spell-checker, word processor) become increasingly important for these writers. But the most powerful tool is language itself. A boy listens to a classmate share a book about Jerry Rice and asks, "Where is this set?" Because this child has the language to refer to setting, he can begin a conversation about this important element of craft. Some students may begin to demonstrate their mastery of specific elements of writing. When we see this, we can name the elements for them. In this way, language becomes a tool the student can use to further craft a piece of writing.

Probably more important than *what* students pay attention to is the habit they develop to pay attention. Third graders can learn the importance of a strong and focused lead. By attending to leads, they begin to develop the stance of the writer—one who writes and reads his or her own writing with a sense of purpose and audience. They read with new deliberateness. They know writing has an impact, that there is more than one way to write something. They see the value in trying their ideas out on an audience. With these habits established, they will be ready in future years to apply them to more sophisticated concepts as they learn to manipulate time, hone a focus, and develop their writing voice.

Exercising the Imagination

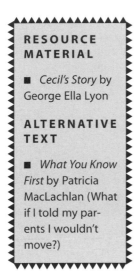

RESOURCE MATERIAL

■ *Cecil's Story* by George Ella Lyon

ALTERNATIVE TEXT

■ *What You Know First* by Patricia MacLachlan (What if I told my parents I wouldn't move?)

DISCUSSION

Writing requires a leap of the imagination. To start with the blank page and end with a story requires the writer to take a mental journey. Too often students get stymied by the "happening truth" of what they are writing about. When students write about actual experiences, they typically lean toward reporting as they concentrate on getting down the facts. When they give themselves permission to invent, they often create fictional stories too big to control. We can help students develop imaginative thinking by providing concrete and deliberate ways they can use it in their writing.

HOW TO TEACH IT

How many of you have ever asked yourself a "what if" kind of question? Perhaps you've found yourself wondering about things you don't know the answer to: What if I had been born before my older brother? What if my dog could talk to me? What if I discovered a shortcut in my backyard that took me all the way to China?

Sometimes writers create a story simply by exploring a single "what if" question. Listen to how George Ella Lyon explores the question, What if my father went to war?

(Read *Cecil's Story.*)

In order to write this simple story the author had to really think about that "what if" question. She didn't try to answer it quickly. Instead she imagined lots of the details of what it might be like and then she wrote them all out in a way that would help the reader imagine it as well.

Do you have a wondering kind of question that has been tugging at you? If so, consider letting it be the subject of a story. You might begin by letting your imagination go to work at answering the question and recording all the possibilities in a notebook or on an idea sheet. Then see if you can shape a story around this one central question.

Using Cut and Paste

RESOURCE MATERIAL

■ Multiple pairs of scissors, rolls of tape, extra paper

■ "A Change in the Weather" (see Appendix 6) (Here is another good, if less dramatic, alternative to story surgery. Take another text where the author has forgotten to include essential information. Show students how to tape a blank piece of paper onto the side. A writer can draw an arrow from the place where the new material is needed to the blank paper, and write it there. In some classrooms the kids cut strips of paper, write what they want to add, and tape these strips onto the margins.)

DISCUSSION

Why don't more kids revise their writing? They sit in the author's chair and answer readers' questions. We make suggestions during writing conferences. We talk about revision until we're blue in the face. Students may be aware *what* their writing needs, but they may not know *how* to weave new material into the text they're working on. Copying the whole thing over may seem like the only solution to many kids. We need to show students concrete ways to incorporate new information into their existing drafts. We need to do everything we can to make it fun, to encourage them to be playful with their revisions.

HOW TO TEACH IT

I want to read the first draft of a story to you.

(Read "A Change in the Weather.")

After I wrote this story, I reread it and asked myself two writer's questions. First, Does it make sense? I think it does. Second, Have I left anything out? Yes, I have. We anchored our boat at an island, and all of a sudden we saw four dolphins. They swam right up to the boat and started surfacing right in front of us. My son put his hand into the water, and the dolphins rubbed against it. Then he told me he wanted to swim with them, and I told him: "You stay in this boat!" He really wanted to jump in with those dolphins.

What do you think—would my story be better if I added the part about the dolphins? I think it would. I think I would add that dolphin part in the middle, probably right here (see asterisk in story). But how do I add that part without going back and recopying the whole thing?

I could do what I call story surgery—take a pair of scissors and cut the story open right at this point. I'm going to tape the top part of my story onto a blank piece of paper.

(Demonstrate.)

Look. I have opened a window into my story. I'll tape this other part of my story down here depending on how much I write. If I write a lot, I'll tape it way down here. I'll need to write first, then tape.

Go back and reread your drafts. Ask yourself those writer's questions. Have you left out anything important? Would you like to try some story surgery on your writing? I've left tape, scissors, and extra paper in the writing center.

"Cracking Open" General Words

RESOURCE MATERIAL

■ "My Stepfather, Rowdy" (see Appendix 7)

DISCUSSION

Vague writing is filled with generalities: "We were goofing around with my dad's stuff." Sharp writing contains precise nouns and specific verbs: "My cousin and I were sword-fighting with Dad's hacksaws." At certain times, a writer needs to use a general word, but young writers typically overdo it.

Here's a craft lesson that can immediately improve students' writing by showing them how to replace generalities with more concrete words and phrases.

HOW TO TEACH IT

Consider the following words: *good, nice, things, stuff, fun.* These are general words. Maybe we can think of other words like them. There's nothing wrong with these words. They have their place, but in writing they don't paint much of a picture. When we read, "My uncle is really fun," we have trouble seeing an image.

As a writer, you can "crack open" a general word like *fun* by using a more specific word. Look what happens when we change the sentence so that it reads, "I had a blast when my uncle took me to a deserted parking lot and let me drive his Jaguar convertible." This sentence creates an image we can see. It tells a great deal about the uncle and exactly what kind of fun took place.

Let's look at this story beginning.

(Read beginning of "My Stepfather, Rowdy.")

You'll find that this story contains a number of vague, general words. Read it over and circle the general words in this piece of writing. You might do this with a friend. How could this writer have "cracked open" these general words to be more specific?

Try the same thing with the story you're working on. Reread it carefully looking for vague, general words. Circle those words. See if you can crack them open and use more precise words to tell the reader exactly what's going on.

Using Stronger Verbs

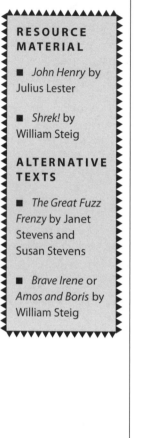

▲▲▲▲▲▲▲▲▲▲▲▲▲

RESOURCE MATERIAL

■ *John Henry* by Julius Lester

■ *Shrek!* by William Steig

ALTERNATIVE TEXTS

■ *The Great Fuzz Frenzy* by Janet Stevens and Susan Stevens

■ *Brave Irene* or *Amos and Boris* by William Steig

▼▼▼▼▼▼▼▼▼▼▼▼▼

DISCUSSION

Teaching students to write well involves helping them unlearn certain formulaic ideas about writing: "Put *said* to bed," and so on. Many students have been taught that their writing will improve if they puff up their sentences with lots of colorful adjectives. Not! In fact, using too many adjectives often leads to verbose, overwritten prose or poetry. If there is a secret to better descriptive writing, it's this: stronger verbs.

HOW TO TEACH IT

You have all studied the parts of speech: nouns, adjectives, verbs, and adverbs. For a writer, this is much more than grammar—these are the bolts and nails you use to build a durable piece of writing.

Here's a simple way to think about nouns and verbs: "The nouns make the pictures, and the verbs make those pictures move." Let's read together excerpts from two books:

Lightning fired his fiercest bolt straight at Shrek's head. Shrek just gobbled it, belched some smoke, and grinned.

John Henry sang and he hammered and the air danced the rainbow shimmered and earth shook and rolled from the blows of the hammer.

Notice the verbs? There are no passive verbs (*is* or *was*) in any of these sentences. The verbs are strong, striking: *fired, gobbled, belched*. These verbs crackle with energy, and they really get the nouns moving: the air *danced*, the rainbow *shimmered*, the earth *shook* and *rolled*.

Today as you revisit your writing I want you to scrutinize your verbs. Did you use too many passive verbs? Are there places where the writing would improve with the use of an active verb instead of a passive one? See if you can't substitute stronger, more precise verbs for any humdrum ones you're currently using.

Unpacking a "Heavy Sentence"

RESOURCE MATERIAL

■ Large chart

■ *The Hello, Goodbye Window* by Norton Juster

ALTERNATIVE TEXTS

■ Kevin Henkes's books—*Lilly's Purple Plastic Purse*; *Julius, the Baby of the World*; *Chester's Way*; *Chrysanthemum*; and others—all show examples of unpacked heavy sentences.

■ *A Seed Is Sleepy* and *An Egg Is Quiet* by Dianna Hutts Aston also show examples.

DISCUSSION

Third and fourth graders are notorious for giving equal weight to every aspect of their writing: "I woke up in the morning. My sister was being a real pain. I went downstairs. I had the worst day of my life in school. The good thing was that I got to have baseball practice after school."

Only the writer knows which part of the story deserves extra attention. But we can help children identify those sentences that are laden with hidden meaning. Then the writer can return to those sentences, unpack them, and flesh them out.

HOW TO TEACH IT

Have you ever noticed how sometimes when you read a story you come to a sentence that makes you eager to know more? Some sentences have a lot of ideas packed inside them. You just know that if you were able to open them like a suitcase there would be lots of interesting things inside.

In his book *The Hello, Goodbye Window*, Norton Juster introduces the window with this sentence: "It looks like a regular window, but it's not." That's a heavy sentence because you just know there are lots of ideas inside it. Later the author writes that Poppy can play only one song on his harmonica, but then adds another heavy sentence: "But he can play it a lot of different ways." This time Norton doesn't make you guess about what is inside that sentence. He opens it up and shows you:

(Draw a vertical line down a chart. On the left side write the heavy sentence. On the other, write the unpacked sentences.)

But he can play it a lot of different ways.	He can play it slow or fast or he can play it sitting down or standing up. He says he can even play it and drink a glass of water at the same time, but I've never seen him do that.

Go back and read what you have written. Put a star next to a sentence that feels heavy, where you feel you might have more to say. How can you unpack it for the reader? What details and examples can you give?

Using Sensory Details

RESOURCE MATERIAL

■ Large chart

Any of these books will work for this lesson.

■ *Working Cotton* by Sherley Anne Williams

■ *Night in the Country* by Cynthia Rylant

■ *Owl Moon* by Jane Yolen

■ *Twilight Comes Twice* by Ralph Fletcher

■ *The Leaving Morning* by Angela Johnson

DISCUSSION

With their newfound fluency, third- and fourth-grade writers typically bolt down the page. Their exciting narratives tend to be plot-heavy but skimpy on description. As writing teachers, we need to slow them down. We need to remind students that the five senses are important tools for making the world of words come alive for the reader.

There are hundreds of wonderful books that illustrate a strong use of sensory detail. We have suggested a few in this lesson, but you may prefer to draw on some favorites of your own.

HOW TO TEACH IT

You might think of the five senses as nets to catch the world. Good writers use these five senses—sight, touch, smell, taste, sound—to bring the world of their stories to their readers.

(You might categorize these sensory details on a large chart or on separate pieces of paper.)

I'm going to read you this picture book. Pay attention to which of the five senses the author uses in the writing.

(Read aloud.)

Which of the senses did the author use to describe something?

As you write your stories, imagine that you're making a movie. I'm in the front row with the rest of your readers, eating our popcorn, watching closely. Not only watching—smelling, touching, tasting, feeling. When you write, use your senses when you describe something. The details you put into your story will help us know exactly what is going on.

Today I'd like you to reread your writing and look at which of the five senses you tend to use the most. Do you use lots of dialogue (sound)? Do you use mostly visual descriptions? See if you can vary the kind of sensory descriptions you use in your writing.

Finding Voice in the World Around Us

RESOURCE MATERIAL

■ Each sign printed on its own chart paper

DISCUSSION

Teaching third and fourth graders to breathe voice into their writing can be a challenge. Not to mention that it's no small task finding words to define this elusive quality. An easy first step is simply making students aware of the sound of voice in writing. Before turning to examples in literature, try this lesson, which uses examples from a comfortable and familiar kind of writing—signs—to help tune your students' ears to voice.

HOW TO TEACH IT

I was sitting at a table eating my lunch when my eye caught a sign taped to the front of a trash container. It read:

Toss it in. Drop it in.
Slide it in off your tray.
Just get your trash
in here some way.

The sign surprised me and made me smile. How different than simply saying: Put Trash Here. (Write the voiceless alternative next to or below the sign filled with voice.) This sign got me to clear my table. How could it not? I could practically hear the clean-up crew pleading with me.

This is an example of the writer's voice. Listening for voice in writing—even simple writing such as signs—will make it easier to bring voice into your own work.

Here's another sign I saw taped to a garage door at my car mechanic's shop:

No Parking
at anytime.
Don't even
think about it.

The sign might have simply said, No Parking. (Again, write this alternative next to the printed sign so students can compare the two.) The sign really made me take notice. When something has strong voice it sticks in your brain and makes you think more about it. Voice does that for readers.

Be on the lookout for samples of voice, not just in the stories and books we read, but in the writing you see in all kinds of places: signs, cereal boxes, instructions, letters, newspaper or magazine headlines. When you find one, jot it down and bring it to class. We'll collect and listen to them together.

Writing with Voice

▲▲▲▲▲▲▲▲▲▲▲▲▲▲

RESOURCE MATERIAL

■ The writing of other students in the class

■ *Honey, I Love* by Eloise Greenfield

■ *Stevie* by John Steptoe

■ *Danny, the Champion of the World* by Roald Dahl

ALTERNATIVE TEXT

■ *Uncle Jed's Barbershop* by Margaree King Mitchell

▼▼▼▼▼▼▼▼▼▼▼▼▼▼

DISCUSSION

Some writing has a spark, a quirky humanness that makes us know beyond doubt that the author is a real person talking to us. This quality is known as voice. By third and fourth grade we can begin talking about this concept. But—alas!—it is just at this point that teachers pile on so many skills expectations that many young writers begin to lose the fresh voice they had as primary writers.

Pat Meehan teaches third grade in Northbrook, Illinois. She says that teaching students to write with voice is a major goal during the year. "They may not be old enough to appreciate voice in their own writing, but they can sense it in the literature they read because that's when you can't pry them away from their reader's trance."

HOW TO TEACH IT

"What makes your writing different from anyone else's?" Pat asks her students. "Are there certain ways that you can recognize an author you like? Is there something that draws you to a particular author? A good writer can capture your attention in many ways; however, there is one quality that stands above the rest. It is voice. It is this quality that reveals the author's true self. It is hers only, the personal style that makes her the author she is. It is the ability of the author to express herself honestly. It is her secret for grabbing the audience, for revealing herself. Donald Murray [1996] says, 'It is the voice that attracts us to the story and makes us believe or not believe it. Voice is the magic that is hard to describe, but it is the most important element in the story, the music that supports and holds the story together' [p. 91].

"I tell my students that a good writer must give part of herself away, must share with her readers if she is to be believed. She must have convictions, be strong, and show passion. She must define herself by speaking sincerely and truly about what she believes. She must shake out her deepest self."

Pat challenges the students to listen for real voice in their own writing: "The evidence for me must be their awareness of showing absolute honesty in their writing—to write from the heart."

Creating a Dramatic Scene

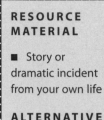

RESOURCE MATERIAL

■ Story or dramatic incident from your own life

ALTERNATIVE TEXTS

■ *Sarah, Plain and Tall* by Patricia MacLachlan

■ *The Stories Julian Tells* by Ann Cameron (or a dramatic scene excerpted from another familiar text)

DISCUSSION

Students in third and fourth grade typically write narrative summaries of events. But there can be a sameness to this kind of writing. One way to get livelier writing is to show students how to craft a dramatic scene. Don't be surprised if some students begin to overuse this powerful tool.

HOW TO TEACH IT

Here's a memory I have from high school:

> When I was eighteen years old my mother told me that she was three months pregnant. I was pretty shocked, since my mother was forty-one at the time.

In this passage the story gets filtered through the narrator (me). I could write this in a different way. I could write a scene that puts the reader smack in the middle of the action, to let the reader see and feel exactly what I saw and felt when I found out the surprising news:

> I saw my mother was on the driveway. She was raking leaves, her strong worn hands clutching the wooden rake. She waved me over.
> "Can I talk to you a second?" she asked. She was smiling, and I noticed a twinkle in her eye I'd never seen before.
> "Sure," I said. "What's up?"
> "I'm three months pregnant," she said. She looked at me, waiting.
> "You're, hey, really?" I sputtered. "Wow! That's good! I mean, that's great! I mean, how do *you* feel about it?"

See the difference? In the first version I summarized what happened. In the second version the narrator doesn't do much talking to the reader. Instead, I described the narrator talking to the mother. I used visual details to describe the driveway and the characters.

Do you have a crucial moment in your story? If you do, that might be a part you could write as a dramatic scene. Think of it as making a movie. You'll want to describe real characters actually doing something. You'll probably want to use dialogue. You'll want to describe the setting. See if you can make your scene come alive.

Summarizing Information

RESOURCE MATERIAL

■ "Learning to Ride My Bike" (see Appendix 8)

DISCUSSION

Writers use details to give a vivid picture of what's going on. But this can be too much of a good thing. A writer can bury readers in so many details that the reader can't figure out which ones are important. A summary can help students avoid this problem.

HOW TO TEACH IT

A friend told me, "Someone tried to rob a cashier at the mall!"

"Really?" I asked.

"See, we were shopping for my friend's Mom. It was her fiftieth birthday, and they were having a big surprise party for her. Relatives were coming from all over the country—"

"Okay, okay," I interrupted. "But what happened at the mall?"

"Well, we were shopping for slippers but it was hard. See, she's got really big feet. In school, the kids used to call her Big Foot. One time when she was in third grade . . ."

My friend was driving me crazy!

When you write, it's important to find the right pacing. There are times when you want to slow down and tell all the juicy details, but there are other times when you want to skip ahead. If you're not careful, you can bury the reader in too many details. If that happens, the reader may get bored and confused, and forget the point of your story.

You can avoid that problem by summarizing. A summary is a writing tool that works a little bit like the fast-forward button on a VCR. It gives readers a short, quick idea of what happened without trying their patience. Summarizing is a way you can quickly give readers less important information they still need to know. A summary is very short—usually just a sentence or two.

Here's a story by a fourth-grade student.

(Read "Learning to Ride My Bike.")

Let's take another look at the last paragraph: "The next few weeks were smothered in blood, scabs, bruises, and Band-Aids . . ." She didn't describe the next time she rode her bike, and the next. That would have been boring. Instead, she gave us a summary of what happened.

Read over your writing. Is there a part where you might be boring your reader with too much detailed description or too much dialogue? I suggest you put a bracket around that part, and write it as a summary.

Sharpening the Focus

RESOURCE MATERIAL

■ *Grandpa's Face* by Eloise Greenfield

■ *Thunder Cake* by Patricia Polacco

■ *Song and Dance Man* by Karen Ackerman

DISCUSSION

By third and fourth grade many writers have built up sufficient fluency to write long, complicated stories. This is an achievement in itself. Students are proud and amazed as the writing goes to three, four, even five pages. But often these students seem incapable of leaving anything out. For these writers, it's time to think about focus—not only the accumulation but also the *selection* of details and events.

"I find that my students want to write everything," Franki Sibberson says about the fourth-grade students she has taught. "Beginning to end, and everything in between. If they do this, their stories don't have much meat. For example, if they write about their grandfather it sounds like a biography, but you really don't get to know the grandfather."

This lesson is similar to "New Ways to Write About an Old Topic" (p. 41) in the K–2 section.

HOW TO TEACH IT

"I usually share lots of books on a single topic," Franki says. "I often use picture books about grandparents. We read lots of them and talk about how the books are about similar topics but are very different stories. We look at each book and see how the author decided on the one story that told the most about his or her grandparent. Through a detailed account of one important story, the reader gets to know the grandparent and the relationship much better than if the author had told everything. Then I ask them to revisit the stories they are working on. Rather than tell everything, I suggest, they should focus on the most important story they want to tell."

Focusing on a Slice of the Pie

RESOURCE MATERIAL

■ Large chart

■ Your own story

DISCUSSION

Without guidance, students will often choose topics that are huge and unfocused: "My Life," "School," or "My Hobbies." No wonder they quickly run out of things to write about! Such topics usually lead to a list of ideas where the writing never goes beneath the surface. Here's one way of modeling for students how to narrow down a large topic.

HOW TO TEACH IT

Writers often start by choosing to write on a big topic: "Summer," "Friends," "My Family." You might think of a topic like "My Family" as an extra-large pizza.

(Draw a large pizza on a chart.)

I run into a problem if I try to write about such a big topic—too many relatives! Where should I start? I could write about the whole topic, but I might have better luck if I focus on a slice of the pie. Here's how I'd do it. I'd ask myself, "Who is one person in my family who's really special to me?" When I ask myself that question I know the answer: my grandfather. I could write about him.

(Draw a slice in the circle.)

I'm starting to narrow down my topic. But the problem is that Grandpa is a big topic. So now I ask myself, "What is one special memory I have of Grandpa?" I remember the time he took me to the park. It started to rain but we didn't leave. We both got soaked. We loved it—we couldn't stop laughing. That's what I'm going to write about. See what's happened? Now I'm taking a slice of the slice. I focused it twice.

(Show a section of the slice.)

Think about this when you write today. Are you trying to eat the whole pizza? Have you picked a topic that's too big? Instead of writing about the whole thing, see if you can focus on a slice of the pie.

Time Focus

▲▲▲▲▲▲▲▲▲▲▲▲▲

RESOURCE MATERIAL

■ *Working Cotton* by Sherley Anne Williams

■ *Birthday Presents* by Cynthia Rylant

ALTERNATIVE TEXTS

■ *Cookie's Week* by Cindy Ward (days of the week)

■ *My Mama Had a Dancing Heart* by Libba Moore Gray (seasons of the year)

■ *Pond Year* by Kathryn Lasky (months of the year)

▼▼▼▼▼▼▼▼▼▼▼▼▼

DISCUSSION

Good writing has a clear sense of focus. Writing is sometimes focused around a central theme; at other times writers employ a specific time frame to narrow in on a topic. Time-focused stories may be structured around natural units of time—a single day, a year in a life—or they may be built to incorporate rituals that recur in the natural order of things—bedtime, birthdays.

HOW TO TEACH IT

Yesterday [in the previous craft lesson] we talked about how a story might take place in just one small slice of a day. Today we're going to look at two books that focus themselves according to a specific period of time. But each does this in a slightly different way.

First, consider *Working Cotton*. Listen to the beginning and the end. Together they signal to us how much time passes in the story.

> We gets to the fields early, before it's even light . . . The bus comes when it's almost dark. Us all be tired.

You can see that this story tells about one single day.
(We find it helpful to provide a visual map of this for students. You could do this with a time line.)

———————————————————————————————
Arriving at the field   Leaving to go home

In Cynthia Rylant's book *Birthday Presents*, more time passes. In fact, six years go by. But Rylant still uses a narrow time focus by showing us only one day of each of the years—the girl's birthday.

————— ————— ————— ————— ————— ———
Real birthday   1ˢᵗ birthday   2ⁿᵈ birthday   3ʳᵈ birthday   4ᵗʰ birthday   etc.

Think about time as you write. Focusing around some element of time will help you decide what to include and what to leave out of your writing.

Narrowing the Time Focus

RESOURCE MATERIAL

■ Story/incident from your own life

■ "Waking Joseph" (see Appendix 9)

ALTERNATIVE TEXTS

These books demonstrate a narrow time focus.

■ *Owl Moon* by Jane Yolen

■ *The Paperboy* by Dav Pilkey

■ *Twilight Comes Twice* by Ralph Fletcher

■ *The Leaving Morning* by Angela Johnson

■ *A South African Night* by Rachel Isadora

DISCUSSION

Time is a tough one. It's hard for kids to be planful in their lives, and it's just as hard for them to handle the time element in their writing. By third and fourth grade we can start showing students various ways of playing with time in their writing.

This craft lesson shows how even a few minutes can give you enough to write an entire piece. Barry Lane calls this "exploding a moment" in his book *After the End* (1993). Narrowing the time focus allows the writer to go deeper into the subject.

HOW TO TEACH IT

Writers make decisions. Out of all the people in the world, you choose your characters. Out of all the places in the world, you select your setting. And you select your time focus, too. Is your story about a weekend, a day, a few hours? Time focus is important. It's much easier to write about your favorite ride at Disney World than it is to describe your whole vacation. You can find enough material for a piece of writing in just a few minutes of time. Let me share this story about someone trying to get his four-year-old son out of bed.

(Read "Waking Joseph.")

Think about the time focus in the piece you are working on. Have you bitten off more time than you can chew? If you are trying to cover too much time in one piece of writing, you might find yourself listing: we did this, then we did this. You might get better results by slowing down and focusing on one small slice of time.

Using Paragraphs to Organize Your Writing

RESOURCE MATERIAL

■ "Sleepover Party" (Appendixes 10 and 11)

DISCUSSION

By the time kids are comfortably reading chapter books, they are ready to learn about paragraphs. As readers, they understand that paragraphs organize information and, as a result, ease the effort of the reader. Here we ask them to think about using this skill as they write.

HOW TO TEACH IT

When I look at your writing I find a lot of good ideas, but it's often hard to read because you've written it all in one big block of print. Writers break up the text into paragraphs or chunks of sentences that connect around a central idea. When you do this, you create white space on the page, and this white space makes it easier for readers to move from one idea to another.

Here's a story that hasn't been organized into paragraphs yet.

(Show "Sleepover Party" from Appendix 10.)

Let's read it together and listen for when the writer shifts from one big idea to another.

(Read "Sleepover Party," noting each time the writer moves from one idea to another. You'll find four potential paragraphs for each of the following main ideas: getting ready for the sleepover, making a mess in the bathroom, trouble falling asleep, and the morning after.)

(Circle each chunk of text to show where the paragraph breaks would be made. Then show students the same story, written in paragraph form from Appendix 11.)

In this second version, you can see that the writer indented from the margin at the start of each paragraph. This signals the reader that the writer is moving from one idea to another.

When you write, think about making new paragraphs each time you shift from one main idea to another. You'll find that this not only helps the reader—it will also help you organize your ideas.

Describing the Setting

RESOURCE MATERIAL

- *Marshfield Dreams* by Ralph Fletcher

- *Working Cotton* by Sherley Anne Williams

ALTERNATIVE TEXTS

- *Going North* by Janice N. Harrington

- *Scarecrow* by Cynthia Rylant

- *The Most Beautiful Place in the World* by Ann Cameron

DISCUSSION

Have you ever noticed that when students write about vacations they usually include little information to create a sense of place? They begin paying attention to the setting by naming it in their writing. You see this when children write about places they have visited (e.g., "My family went skiing in Colorado"). But all stories have settings. Some are as familiar as one's own backyard, while others may be as exotic as a rodeo. Once students can name the setting of a story, they can include description in order to develop the story's sense of place.

HOW TO TEACH IT

All stories take place somewhere. Any story you are writing—whether true or fiction—happens in some particular place. A story might be set at the beach; another might take place in a shopping mall. Writers talk about this as the setting of the story. Often they include a description of the place so the reader can get a feel for the story's setting. Let's consider some books we've read lately. Let's look at where the story takes place and then at some description the writer uses to tell about the setting.

Book	Setting	Description
Marshfield Dreams	The swamp	I loved the dank smell of that swamp and all the things that lived there: mossy logs and goggle-eyed frogs, blood-suckers and eels and foul-smelling skunk cabbage. Half the swamp was under water, and the other half contained thick, dense mud. It was impossible to walk through that mud without getting stuck.
Working Cotton	In the farm fields	The field fire send up a gray trail to the hazy sky. The rows of cotton stretch far as I can see.

Where does your story take place? What description could you include to help a reader get a sense of that place?

Copyright © 2007

Ralph Fletcher and

JoAnn Portalupi.

Stenhouse Publishers

Describing a Character

DISCUSSION

A writer needs to describe a character so we can get a picture in our minds. So why don't more young writers do it? It may be that writing workshops have leaned too hard (and for too long) on personal narrative writing. Personal narrative is very important, but if a student can mentally picture the brother or uncle he is writing about, he may not feel the need to give readers the visual clues necessary so we can picture the same character. In this craft lesson we suggest a strategy for describing a character the reader can picture.

HOW TO TEACH IT

In a good piece of writing, the characters come alive. We feel like we know them, we care about them, and they become part of who we are. If you want your readers to care about your characters, they have to be able to picture them. In a picture book you can draw the characters. But in a story you have to include enough written description so we can picture them.

Let's revisit *The Barn* by Avi. You remember that Benjamin comes from school when his father has a stroke. This is how Avi describes Father when Benjamin first comes home to see him:

> The last time I had seen him, he was tall and strong. The only thing he'd never owed money on, he'd say, was his handsome face, and Mother bought it right off the shelf.
>
> Now that same face showed nothing but sick and sour dirtiness. His beard—about which he'd been so vain and about which I teased him often in fun—was all crossways, as was his gray-streaked hair.
>
> He made me think of an old corn husk doll without stuffing. As I stood staring, he made fluttering motions at the coverlet, his fingers jumping like small fish hauled to land.

Go back and revisit the writing you're working on. Have you given your reader enough description so we can picture whom you're writing about? Is your character tall or pudgy? Hairy or bald? Have you included physical details so we can tell? If not, you might begin by using a separate piece of paper to describe this character. Would the description make the writing stronger? Where would you insert it in your text?

The Inner Life of a Character

RESOURCE MATERIAL

■ "Spot" (see Appendix 12)

ALTERNATIVE TEXTS

These texts have a strong sense of a character's inner life:

■ "Slower Than the Rest" by Cynthia Rylant

■ *A Tiger Called Thomas* by Charlotte Zolotow

■ *Tar Beach* by Faith Ringgold

DISCUSSION

Too often we have this reaction when we finish reading a piece of writing: So what? What's the point? Why is this important?

Often the reader has no sense of a character's inner life. It's hard for the reader to care for a character like this. But once a writer lets us into that inner world—thoughts, feelings, conflicts—we can begin to understand the particular meaning or significance of an event. This is a stretch for some third and fourth graders. But we can begin by making them aware of a character's inner life.

HOW TO TEACH IT

Stories are about what happens to characters. But stories are also about what happens *inside* these characters. All of us have thoughts, dreams, and feelings. You might share them with a friend, or a special grown-up, or you might just keep them to yourself. Either way, the things that are happening on the inside have a definite effect on what is happening on the outside.

I'm going to read to you a story by a third grader named Wade. The main character in this story is a boy named Dave. Pay attention to the way the author lets us peek into Dave's inner life.

(Read "Spot." Discuss.)

There is a lot going on in this simple story. By telling us how Dave is feeling in the first half of the story, Wade sets up what happens in the second half. Try to imagine how the story would read if the first part were left out. Imagine if the story began, "In two more days it would be Christmas. The two days had passed . . ." If we didn't know how lonely Dave was, we wouldn't be able to understand the importance to him of getting that new puppy.

Think of the characters in your story. Do you give the reader a peek into the inner lives of your characters? Do we know how they are feeling? Maybe you are the main character in your story. How could you let the reader know how you're feeling, and what you're thinking about?

Person Versus Nature

RESOURCE MATERIAL

■ *Brave Irene* by William Steig

ALTERNATIVE TEXT

■ *Hatchet* by Gary Paulsen

DISCUSSION

This kind of conflict grows naturally out of writing in which there is a strong sense of setting, of place. Unfortunately, the available models from the media tend to be high-budget Hollywood extravaganzas (*Twister*, *Volcano*, *Jaws*, and so on). Such films will not steer young writers toward smaller, more manageable topics.

When the person versus nature conflict works well in a piece of writing, the main character undergoes some kind of change or transformation. The challenge forces him or her to reach deep inside to summon the strength to overcome it. The writer, then, has to find a way to take us inside the character. Make sure your students are familiar with *Brave Irene*, a well-known picture book by William Steig. The person versus nature conflict makes it a good one to study in depth when exploring this element of craft.

HOW TO TEACH IT

By the second page of *Brave Irene* we know that Irene is a determined character. Even though Irene's mother is sick, and a snowstorm has begun, Irene decides to deliver the dress to the duchess herself. But the moment she steps outside Irene realizes that this won't be easy. And it isn't. Steig shows lots of big and little ways the wind gets in Irene's way. It hurries her along, blows snow into her boots, tries to wrest the package from her grip. Irene and the wind match wits with each other. At one point the wind seems to become a person, and Irene actually argues with it:

> "Go home!" the wind squalled. "Irene . . . go hooooooome . . ."
> "I will do no such thing," she snapped. "No such thing, you wicked wind!"
> "Go ho-o-ome," the wind yodeled. "GO HO-WO-WOME," it shrieked, "or else."

(Discuss with your students the different ways Steig builds the conflict between girl and blizzard. You might create a chart for this purpose to list the sensory details. Things get worse for Irene before they get better. This is true for many stories where the main conflict is person versus nature.)

Some of you may have this kind of conflict in the story you're working on. If you do, you can try out some of the techniques Steig uses in *Brave Irene*. If you don't, consider using this conflict in your writing in the future.

Using a Parallel Story

RESOURCE MATERIAL

■ *The Paperboy* by Dav Pilkey

■ "Slower Than the Rest" by Cynthia Rylant

ALTERNATIVE TEXT

■ *Henry Hikes to Fitchburg* by D. B. Johnson

DISCUSSION

This writing technique sounds sophisticated, and it may be a stretch for some third or fourth graders. But this strategy is easy to explain, and there are many accessible texts available to model it. There's no reason why students can't study how professional writers use this strategy, and experiment with it themselves in their own writing. (Of course, not all students will do so.)

In the text that follows we discuss how you can use a picture book as well as a short story to model this craft lesson.

HOW TO TEACH IT

Dav Pilkey uses a parallel story in his picture book *The Paperboy*. All through this book we see the boy doing one thing and the dog doing something similar. They don't do exactly the same things—a dog can't ride a bike or put rubber bands on folded newspapers—but there are enough similarities to make the point. Pilkey is an author/illustrator, so he can show the parallel stories in both the illustrations and the text, for example, when he shows both boy and dog eating breakfast from their different bowls.

The Paperboy reveals some interesting truths about books with parallel stories. Two characters are being compared, but they don't do exactly the same things. The characters' parallel stories are different enough to make the story interesting.

"Slower Than the Rest" is a short story by Cynthia Rylant. The main character is Leo, who is a "slow" kid in school. He takes a long time understanding his subjects, so he has been placed in a special class. While driving with his family, Leo finds a turtle and names him Charlie. Leo brings Charlie to school and gives a wonderful report on turtles. In this way, he finally gets appreciated.

(After students reread this story, talk with them about all the ways that Cynthia Rylant compares the boy with the turtle. There are a number of concrete references in the text. Invite them to try a parallel story in their own writing.)

Crafting a Lead

RESOURCE MATERIAL

■ *Wilma Unlimited* by Kathleen Krull

ALTERNATIVE TEXTS

■ *The Two of Them* by Aliki

■ *Uncle Jed's Barbershop* by Margaree King Mitchell

DISCUSSION

Many students begin writing with a first sentence that summarizes the entire story: "Last year I got a new puppy for Christmas, and that was the best present I ever got in my whole life." This craft lesson shows an alternative to the summarizing lead.

HOW TO TEACH IT

Let's look at two different ways to begin a story. This is the lead Kathleen Krull used in her book *Wilma Unlimited*:

> No one expected such a tiny girl to have a first birthday. In Clarksville, Tennessee, in 1940, life for a baby who weighed just over four pounds at birth was sure to be limited.
>   But most babies didn't have nineteen older brothers and sisters to watch over them. Most babies didn't have a mother who knew home remedies and a father who worked several jobs.
>   Most babies weren't Wilma Rudolph.

Now let's consider another possible beginning:

> Wilma Rudolph fought against all odds to become the first American woman to win three gold medals in an Olympic competition.

This last lead summarizes the whole story of Wilma Rudolph's life. The first lead—the one Krull chose to write—gives information about young Wilma that makes us begin to wonder who she is and what will happen in her life. It's not always wise to reveal too early the main event of a story. Sometimes a better approach is to write a lead that allows the reader to experience the story as it unfolds.

Today I'd like you to look at your opening sentences and see whether you have written a lead that summarizes. Often you write a summary lead without really planning to. It happens because you are thinking hard about your topic and it just comes out. Think about which kind of lead would work best for the story you are writing. You may want to write a lead that suggests what is to come instead of blurting it out all at once.

Copyright © 2007
Ralph Fletcher and
JoAnn Portalupi.
Stenhouse Publishers

The Give-Away Lead

RESOURCE MATERIAL

■ *Louis the Fish* by Arthur Yorinks

ALTERNATIVE TEXTS

■ *Old Yeller* by Fred Gipson

■ *Mick Harte Was Here* by Barbara Park

DISCUSSION

Students will develop their tastes as readers, and their styles as writers, by recognizing and appreciating the various ways writers approach their topics. In the last craft lesson we talk about the use of suggestion in opening a piece of writing. Sometimes authors take an opposite approach and give away the end of the story right up front. This kind of lead creates a different kind of tension that keeps you reading.

HOW TO TEACH IT

Last week we talked about leads that suggest or give clues compared to those leads that give a summary of the story. Today we're going to look at a book, *Louis the Fish*, where the author uses a summary lead in a way that really works. In fact, it might be better to call this a "give-away lead" because it actually gives away the ending of the story.
Listen to the book's outrageous opening sentence:

One day last spring, Louis, a butcher, turned into a fish. Big lips. A tail. A salmon.

Arthur Yorinks sums up the story in the first few sentences. But rather than give the story away, the lead only makes us curious to read on to see how such a thing could happen. The whole time we are reading about Louis, we wonder how he will change from a person into a big, silvery salmon. Our curiosity keeps us reading.
Sometimes the best way to start a piece of writing is with a give-away lead. That will depend on what you are writing about and whether or not the story becomes more interesting if you know the ending in advance. Take a look at the piece you are working on. Is it possible that the give-away lead would work for you here? If so, try it and see what happens.

Craft Lessons: Teaching Writing K–8 **SECOND EDITION**

Developing the Middle

RESOURCE MATERIAL

■ Large chart

■ *Scarecrow* by Cynthia Rylant

ALTERNATIVE TEXT

■ *Now One Foot, Now the Other* by Tomie de Paola

DISCUSSION

We need to help students know what fits in the middle of a piece of writing, and how to develop that part. We borrowed this craft lesson from Julie Leal, a writing teacher in Texas.

HOW TO TEACH IT

Any piece of writing has a beginning, a middle, and an end. The lead is an important way to grab the reader. The ending is the last thing that will linger in the reader's ear. But what about the middle? The middle is the body—the juice, the meat—that contains the main part of the report, poem, or story you are working on.

Let's take a look at *Scarecrow*, a picture book by Cynthia Rylant. (Read *Scarecrow*.)

What struck you about this book? (Discuss.)

I'm going to read it again. This time I want you to notice the different parts of the book: the beginning, the middle, and the end.

(Read *Scarecrow* again.)

Where does the beginning seem to end, and the middle part start? (Discuss. Kids may notice that the beginning probably ends on p. 2.)

What things did the author put into the middle of the story? (Discuss and prepare to write on a chart.)

Let's think of the things she describes in the middle:

1. The character of the scarecrow: his thoughts and temperament
2. The birds that don't seem afraid of him
3. The setting—all the things growing and happening around him

Finally, where do you think the ending begins? (Discuss.)

Each of these parts gives Cynthia Rylant a way to flesh out her story, to elaborate on the life of a scarecrow.

Think of the writing you're working on. What is the middle part? The middle is probably the most important, so that should probably be the longest part. What could you add (thoughts, feelings, specific details) to flesh out the middle and make it more interesting to the reader?

Staying on Topic

▲▲▲▲▲▲▲▲▲▲▲▲▲

RESOURCE MATERIAL

■ "The Salt Marsh (Appendix 13) copied for students or printed on a chart

▼▼▼▼▼▼▼▼▼▼▼▼▼

DISCUSSION

The goal of this lesson is to help students become more skillful at rereading what they have written. Here we ask students to reflect on what they have written to decide: what is important? What is not?

Don't be surprised if they have difficulty in making this distinction when looking at their writing. Students may do this poorly before they learn how to do it well.

HOW TO TEACH IT

Writers reread. After you have written a rough draft you need to stand back, take a deep breath, and reread what you have written. As you do this you should ask yourself: Which parts are important to what I'm writing about? Where have I wandered away from my topic? All writers drift away from the main idea every so often. The trick is to catch yourself when you do it.

Let's take a look at a piece of writing titled "The Salt Marsh." As we read it together, pay attention to where this writer stays on his topic, and where he wanders away from it.

(Read "The Salt Marsh." Discuss.)

Where did the writer start talking about something that had nothing to do with the salt marsh?

(Discuss. Students may point out the parts about Mike Marsh, the "Breakfast Bullet," and when the writer talks about disliking diet soda.)

When you find places where you've written off topic, you have a few choices. You can simply draw a line through those sentences. Or, you can use a highlighter to mark them. Later, when you do another draft, make sure you leave those parts out. When you revise, your writing will be stronger if you cut those sections that don't belong.

Sometimes those are some of your favorite parts, and it can be hard to cut them, but don't worry—you can always use the parts you left out in another piece of writing.

Experiment with Endings

RESOURCE MATERIAL

- *Fig Pudding* by Ralph Fletcher

ALTERNATIVE TEXTS

The following books offer a variety of endings:

- *Coming on Home Soon* by Jacqueline Woodson (use of title as ending)

- *The Gardener* by Sarah Stewart (using illustrations to end beyond the words)

- *Smoky Night* by Eve Bunting (ending on a small but significant detail)

DISCUSSION

The ending just may be the most important part in a piece of writing. The final words leave a lasting impression on the reader. But coming up with the right ending is hard. Students often use the same ending over and over again: "I woke up and found that it was just a dream." Or: "That's All, Folks!" Or (in large letters): THE END.

"Third graders are always in the middle," says Pat Meehan, a third-grade teacher in Northbrook, Illinois. "They're in the middle of trying to be responsible in school. Parents expect them to know all the conventions of perfect spelling in their writing, but they're caught in the middle of understanding the art of good writing and trying it out. They also *write* in the middle. They really don't use beginnings or endings. And I think one reason is because they don't use a beginning or ending when they *tell* their stories, either."

HOW TO TEACH IT

Pat begins by raising her students' awareness of various kinds of endings. Then she challenges them to rethink the way they have been ending their writing: "'Could you come up with something better?'

"I point out to my students that often they write only the middle of the story. I explain that in writing we must leave one room first before we can enter another. Otherwise we can become lost, as if we were in a maze of pathways without doors.

"I read aloud the ending of a story or book that is familiar to students. I often use 'The Tackle Box' chapter in *Fig Pudding*. The ending—'It seemed like a small price to pay'—shows an alternative to typical third-grade endings.

"I ask students to find several different ending types, and enter them into their writing notebooks. Sticky notes are handy for collecting. The students keep pads out all the time, and enjoy filling up their desktops with examples. Later they can add them or just paste them into their writer's notebooks."

The Circular Ending

RESOURCE MATERIAL

■ "My Grandpa" (see Appendix 14)

ALTERNATIVE TEXTS

■ *The Lotus Seed* by Sherry Garland

■ *The Paperboy* by Dav Pilkey

■ "Poem" by Langston Hughes

DISCUSSION

We have urged our students to write strong leads, but we haven't given the same emphasis to what happens at the end of the piece. Endings matter. We need to model different options for our students so they can see the range of possibilities for ending their writing. The circular ending is a practical alternative to THE END or "That's All, Folks!"

HOW TO TEACH IT

Writers work hard to find the right shape for a story or poem. Some stories build to a dramatic conclusion at the end. Other stories use a circular ending—it circles back to the way it began. Look at this poem by Jeanine, a third-grade writer.

(Display the poem, "My Grandpa," so kids can see it.)

It's interesting to see how a circular ending works. When I read the first line in this poem—"My grandpa is not around"—it makes me feel only a little bit sad because at this point I don't really know anything about the grandfather. Then I read all the things he did for the girl. This writer shows me examples of exactly how he cared for her. The grandfather was a doctor, so he actually delivered the girl when she was born!

It's a whole different experience when I read that line—"My grandpa is not around"—at the very end. When I read that line the second time, I feel a full dose of sadness. And love.

Jeanine uses a circular ending in her poem, but you can also use it in a story or even an informational report. This kind of ending gives the writing balance by using the same thing at the beginning and at the end. In this way it pulls the piece together.

Keep this in mind when you write the ending to the piece you're working on. Don't force it. Circular endings won't work in every piece of writing. If you want to try it, first select the right detail or sentence that you'll come back to at the very end.

Emotional Endings

DISCUSSION

Our students have emotional experiences they can tap in their writing. As writing teachers, we need to create the kind of environment where students are comfortable sharing both good and bad experiences. As they expand the emotional range of their stories, we can show them new ways to end those stories. There's no better way to model this than through a student's writing.

HOW TO TEACH IT

As a writer, you have lots of choices when you try to decide how you want your story to end. You can write an ending that is funny, one that's happy, or one that's sad. Here's a tip: try to match the kind of ending with the kind of story you are writing. You want to leave the reader with the same strong feeling you had when the story happened to you.

Let me share this story that was written by Derek, a second-grade writer from Georgia.

(Read "My Pet Dog.")

Let's take another look at how Derek ended his story.

(Reread.)

Derek wrote a sad story, and he wrote an ending to fit with his story.

Remember: the ending is very important because it's the last thing that echoes in the ear of the reader. Think about the story you're working on, or the kind of story you want to write. You may want to write a story that has strong feelings in it. If you do, you'll probably want to come up with an ending that matches the kind of story you have written.

Surprise Endings

▲▲▲▲▲▲▲▲▲▲▲▲▲

RESOURCE MATERIAL

■ *Charlie Anderson* by Barbara Abercrombie

ALTERNATIVE TEXT

■ *White Dynamite and Curly Kidd* by Bill Martin, Jr. and John Archambault

▼▼▼▼▼▼▼▼▼▼▼▼▼

DISCUSSION

There's nothing quite so delicious as a surprise ending. People delight in the surprise ending to a movie, joke, story, or novel. Students are willing and even eager to try this type of ending in their own work. But, of course, there's a catch. Surprise endings may look easy to pull off, but they're not. More often than not they sound clunky and arbitrary when young writers try them.

Students need our guidance. And more than that, they need our patience when their results don't turn out quite as wonderfully as they (and we) might have hoped.

HOW TO TEACH IT

We've talked about circular endings, and some of you have used that technique in your writing. Today I want to explore with you a different kind of ending. Let's revisit a picture book we all know.

(Read *Charlie Anderson* or summarize it and remind them how the story ends.)

That's a surprise ending—I wonder if you were as surprised by that ending as I was! Some of you might want to try a surprise ending in your own writing. Here are a few things to think about.

Jane Yolen says that the seeds for a surprise ending usually get planted earlier in the story. In other words, you can't just spring the surprise on the reader. First you have to set it up. In *Charlie Anderson*, the author mentions earlier that the girls' parents were divorced. This page (show) sets up the very last page (show). Without this first page, the ending doesn't make sense.

Have you thought of trying a surprise ending in your writing? First, you have to decide if a surprise ending will fit the story you're working on. Think about how you're going to make it work. You might decide to write the surprise ending first. Then you can go back and insert the details or clues to make the ending work.

Crafting a Title

RESOURCE MATERIAL

■ *My Rotten Redheaded Older Brother* by Patricia Polacco

■ *Sarah, Plain and Tall* by Patricia MacLachlan

■ *Smoky Night* by Eve Bunting

■ *Grandfather's Journey* by Allen Say

DISCUSSION

Some students slap a title on the top of the paper as their first act of writing. While these titles serve as a doorway into the story for the writer, they often fall short of the work they could do for the reader. Crafting the title is an important part of writing an effective text. Like a good lead, the title invites the reader into the story. It sets the tone and expectations for what will follow.

HOW TO TEACH IT

I want to talk with you today about titles. I think of the title as a doorway into the story. Many of you write the title at the beginning before the story is written. When you write the title at this point, it's like the title is a doorway for the writer. It helps you enter the story; it makes it easier to get started. But often you discover the meaning and design of a story as you are writing it. You discover the focus or the perfect ending. A special line occurs that you decide to repeat. Once you have finished the story, it's good to reconsider the title and ask yourself, "Is this title a good doorway for the reader?"

The title might point to the important character in a story, as in *My Rotten Redheaded Older Brother* or *Sarah, Plain and Tall*. Sometimes the title refers to a central event, as in *Smoky Night* or *Grandfather's Journey*.

One way to craft a title is to generate a list of different choices—say eight to ten. Then imagine that you are the reader. What does each title suggest about the story to follow? Is that the doorway you want the reader to enter?

Ask yourself if you are almost to the point of finishing a piece of writing. If so, this may be a good time for you to go back and reconsider the title in order to make it just right.

Writing a Title to Preserve the Mystery

RESOURCE MATERIAL

■ Your own story

DISCUSSION

Titles matter. Like a lead, the title is a first handshake between author and reader. It is a way to pull the reader in or push the reader away.

Some students seem to have a knack for coming up with lively titles: "My Guinea Pig, Escape Artist," or "The Double Baby Day." But other writers get so hung up on the title they get discouraged before they have begun any writing. Still other students find that their titles are no more than lifeless labels. They need our help to fashion the best possible title for their writing.

HOW TO TEACH IT

The title is an important part of your writing. Like the lead, the title can entice your reader or turn that reader off. Your title should give the reader some idea about the main idea of your story. But some titles tell *too* much. Some titles are just labels: "When My Sister Fell Down the Stairs." Listen to this story and think about what its title could be:

> Once I was at the beach with some relatives. My cousin Mark found a huge jellyfish that had washed up on shore. We put it into a tub with water, carried it home, and forgot about it. Later we were playing baseball. My little brother ran back to catch a ball and fell into the basin with the jellyfish! He went underwater and came up screaming. It took a long time to calm him down.

I could title this story "When My Brother Fell in with the Jellyfish." That's what happened, but that title tells the reader too much. Later, when the reader comes to the part where he falls in, the reaction will be, "Oh, yes, I already know about this from the title." My title lessens the shock and horror of the experience. A better title would be less specific: "Cape Cod Nightmare." Or: "Tentacles of Horror."

Don't get hung up on your title when you're just starting to write. But after you've finished, take a closer look. Have you written a label, or a title that tells too much? How could you revise it to preserve the mystery? You might want to get a blank piece of paper and brainstorm four or five titles until you settle on the one that feels right.

Combining Short Sentences

RESOURCE MATERIAL

■ Chart showing sentences, or sentences photocopied

ALTERNATIVE TEXT

■ "Looking at Compound Sentences" (Appendix 16)

DISCUSSION

The purpose of this lesson is to attune students' ear to how their writing sounds. Combining short sentences is a revision strategy tangible enough so that upper elementary students can have success with it.

HOW TO TEACH IT

It sounds funny, but we write with our ear. When you read back what you have written, it's important to listen to how the sentences sound, how the writing flows. Sometimes when you read over your writing you find sentences like this:

> We drove to the Rec Center. It started to rain. My little sister got mad. They closed the pool.

> How does this sound? (Discuss.)

There's nothing wrong with a short sentence—it can be a great way to emphasize an idea, or a moment. But a series of short sentences can sound choppy and interrupt the flow. Each period makes you stop and start again. When you hear this, you may want to smooth those choppy sentences out by combining short sentences—merging them into one. The longer sentence you create is called a compound sentence.

> We drove to the Rec Center, *but* it started to rain. My little sister got mad *when* they closed the pool.

> In order to merge two sentences into one, we needed a connecting word: *but, when.* When you combine sentences, other connecting words can be useful: *after, because, since, so.* Sometimes when you combine two sentences, it makes more sense to reverse their order:

> We went to the beach. We didn't find our friends.
> We didn't find our friends when we went to the beach.

> If you find you have lots of short, choppy sentences in your writing, experiment with combining some of them in the way we discussed.

Craft Lessons 5–8

*W*hen our eldest son, Taylor, was in the fifth grade he was asked to write a research paper for social studies. It was due on the first day back after spring break. The first weekend came and went. Monday and Tuesday passed and still there was no sign of Taylor's starting the project. By Wednesday it was time to say something.

"Taylor, I know your paper isn't due until Monday, but remember, you're not going to write it out perfectly the first time. You'll want to give yourself time to write a draft, read it over, make changes, edit."

He patiently let me finish before saying, "Mom, this isn't writing workshop!"

Like many fifth graders, Taylor didn't see any connection between the writing he was doing in writer's workshop and the writing he was asked to do at other moments of his school day or outside of school. It's no surprise. His thinking was reinforced by the compartmentalized structure of the school day.

As students enter the upper elementary and junior high years they get buried under growing curricular pressures. They face intensified demands to develop subject-matter knowledge in math, reading, and language arts. This leads to an unfortunate paradox: just at the point when students are able to try more challenging strategies in their writing, the teacher suddenly has less time to devote to writing workshop. Writing time often gets usurped to serve other content areas. We can kill two birds with one stone by assigning students to write on topics being studied in other school subjects. But, as Lucy Calkins points out, usually both birds die.

The pressure to cover the curriculum pervades our language arts teaching. In fifth through eighth grade, students become accountable for writing across the range of narrative, expository, persuasive, and descriptive modes. How can we help students learn the way these forms can serve their distinct purposes for writing instead of letting the form serve as an end to their work? We can easily make the mistake of letting the need to "cover" these modes define what we teach students about writing. Instead, we might better serve the dual needs of the developing writer and of the curriculum by first recognizing what students of this age are capable of doing on their own.

Most writers at this age have overcome the obstacles that impede fluency of writing. Yes, there are still issues of spelling and mechanics, but they can be handled quickly, leaving more time and attention directed to content. Because of this, the focus on *what* to say can now be shifted toward *how* to say it. For the first time, students are able to write true second drafts. Where younger students rely on manipulations to revise (cut and paste, arrows and codes), fifth- through eighth-grade writers are able to step away from an attempt, consider a new approach, and start over. These multiple drafts may involve taking a whole new angle (starting at a different point in time, changing the point of view) or they may involve what Donald Murray refers to as layering. A student can work from a first draft to write a new, improved version—elaborating here, slowing down the action there. This kind of shaping demands that much of the work be done internally. The older student can meet the cognitive challenge required to do this.

Long and unwieldy fictional stories are a hallmark of this age. These students cast a wider net and allow the range of fictional genres into their writing. We see more realistic as well as historical fiction. Many students get tangled in long, complicated plots that make it difficult for either student or teacher to manage the piece. Editing a twenty-page paper is a daunting challenge, let alone revising it!

One reason for this may be the models they have to draw on. These students have also become more fluent readers, and it's not uncommon for them to read novels of two hundred pages or more. The stories they watch in film format (another popular model for older writers) would also be lengthy in written form. A close look at these students' fiction shows that they've often chosen a cast of characters and a plot that require many more pages to develop than they are prepared to write. It's no wonder we struggle to help them shoehorn these stories into a mere ten or twelve pages.

This is one of the reasons so many teachers have begun using picture books in upper-grade writing workshops. If you were to strip the illustrations from a book like *Faithful Elephants* by Yukio Tsuchiya (which we wouldn't suggest you actually do), what remains is a text very much the length of the writing your students are asked to do. From this model, students can learn about the size and scope of plot and character development in a way that helps them shape their own stories. Because picture books are short, they are easily rereadable. It is only in the rereading that we begin to notice the nuances of language, the way writers use details to evoke all our senses, the subtleties of what gets explained and what is implied.

You can often tell which students are avid readers because their writing has the sound of book language. True, this occurs with young writers, but as students reach the upper grades they become much more deliberate in their attempts to imitate favorite writers. While a third grader might overuse the exclamation point when she first masters it, a seventh grader might "over-write" in an attempt to describe in detail the outfit of the young girl as she steps out of her horse-drawn carriage. In search of their own writer's voice, students at this age will try on the style of the writers they love and admire. If they don't attempt this on their own, they will often do so with our encouragement.

If your students have been fortunate enough to have grown up in writing-process classrooms where they've been given plenty of time to write, these years are a time to learn new lessons and deepen some old ones. Don't make the mistake of thinking they've had enough of narrative writing. "Been there, done that," teachers often say about personal narrative; it's time to move on. While there are new challenges when we move to different genres, remember that learning to write is no different than learning anything else. When our son Robert wanted to sign up for soccer again this year, we didn't encourage him to try another sport. Yes, he will be playing the same game, but hopefully he'll play it at a more advanced level.

The lessons in this section address issues of craft that cut across genre. Students can apply them to narrative writing as well as to fiction, exposition, or poetry. Either way, they are designed to take students to a new level of the game.

Finding a Focus (1)

▲▲▲▲▲▲▲▲▲▲▲▲▲

RESOURCE MATERIAL

■ *Bigmama's* by Donald Crews

■ *Shortcut* by Donald Crews

■ *Arthur for the Very First Time* by Patricia MacLachlan

■ *Sarah, Plain and Tall* by Patricia MacLachlan

▼▼▼▼▼▼▼▼▼▼▼▼▼

DISCUSSION

We encourage students to *focus*, but we may need to break down this abstract word so they can understand exactly what we're talking about. We need to let students feel the way writing takes on new power when they move from the general to the specific. Here's how Lynn Herschlein teaches it to her fifth graders.

HOW TO TEACH IT

"First, I read *Bigmama's*, by Donald Crews, a collection of Crews's memories of the summers he spent at his grandparents' home. This picture book is more like the whole summer. I tell students that after Crews wrote *Bigmama's*, he decided to write about *one* piece of his summer, one specific memory. He chose to tell about the time he and his cousins took a shortcut along the train tracks.

"*Shortcut* is a moment in time that Crews captures with detail, sound effect, suspense. It reminds kids of the times they dared to do (or at least thought about doing) something dangerous. It's about fear, relief, and keeping a lifelong secret. With my students I call these 'the bigger issues,' and they become used to that distinction—underlying feelings and ideas that run through our experiences rather than the simple happenings of our lives.

"The next day I read *Shortcut* and we talk about the differences between the two books. Why did Crews choose this moment in time to zoom in on?

"The kids have another reference point in having read MacLachlan's *Arthur for the Very First Time*, in which the author mentions a mail-order bride and hints at an interesting character. We find out later that these were the seed ideas that eventually became *Sarah, Plain and Tall*. This leads to a discussion of how writing begets writing, and how we can often surprise ourselves at what comes from an exploration process. I encourage my students to think small in their own personal writing. When the kids write their memoirs, I'm always amazed at what 'threads' they discover in their lives. They begin choosing moments that matter, often small moments."

Finding a Focus (2)

RESOURCE MATERIAL

- Stories from your own life

- Photographs

- Overhead transparency

DISCUSSION

A mini-lesson can create a teachable moment, but Shelley Harwayne warns that the danger in such a brief lesson is mentioning instead of teaching. Focus, for example, is such an important strategy you may need to have several mini-lessons before students begin to make it part of their repertoire as writers. Lynn Herschlein has found that using her own writing based on her life gives her fifth graders another way to understand this idea.

HOW TO TEACH IT

"I share with my students a piece of my own writing, a long piece about my dog from beginning to end. I tell them that I feel frustrated with this piece. It's boring and doesn't capture the essence of who my dog was. It's an example of the whole story with no focus.

"Sometimes I compare focus in writing with taking photographs. I show my students two photos of my daughter, Allison. One is a close-up of her face, and the other is a scenic shot of her standing at the beach. We talk about which photo they prefer to look at, and why.

"Then I ask the kids which part of my dog story they'd like to know more about. We find that part and write the first line at the top of a clean overhead sheet. Then I field questions from my students about that part. I think aloud, make decisions with them about what and how to write in order to capture the moments they want to see, hear, touch, taste.

"During the course of the week, the kids have been reading through their notebooks looking for entries they like or that move them in some way. I ask them to select an entry, topic, or special day, and they write about it for a whole week. Each day they take a different approach, a different point of view, looking for the 'bigger issue,' or just having fun remembering more good stuff. Eventually, they decide on a focus."

Deciding Where to Begin

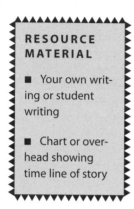

RESOURCE MATERIAL

■ Your own writing or student writing

■ Chart or overhead showing time line of story

DISCUSSION

When students first begin writing personal narratives they have a tendency to let the real time of the experience control the telling of the story. As they develop as writers, they learn how to manipulate time in order to craft a more engaging story. Perhaps the easiest way to start is by having students consider the total time frame of their stories in order to make a deliberate decision of where the story should begin.

HOW TO TEACH IT

When you write a story—whether personal narrative or fiction—one of the elements you have to consider is time. What is the time frame of the story? Will the story take place in an afternoon? a weekend? over the summer?

A strategy that can help you think about time in your story is to lay out a time line of what really happened. If you are writing fiction, you can do this with the sequence of events you have created in your mind. Once the time line is complete, your job is to decide how you will design narrative time in order to create an experience for the reader. The first question you might ask is, Where should the reader enter the story? Where do I want to begin?

(It helps to model this for students. Do this with a story of your own or with student writing. If you have shared this strategy in a conference with an individual writer, you and the student might use that story to demonstrate. Include an example showing a time line of events. Select a number of different starting points on the time line and ask students to consider what it would be like for the reader to start at each of them. Point out to students that they can start anywhere and then use flashback to include any significant scenes from earlier on the time line.)

If you're just beginning a draft, you might make a time line of the events you're writing about. Look over the time line and decide at what point in time you want the story to begin.

Writing the No-Time Narrative

DISCUSSION

Some texts seem to hang in a period of suspended time. We might think of these as hybrids between expository writing and narrative. Younger students often write an "All About" book, such as "All About My Family," that may include six pages of family portraits and related anecdotes. In the overall framework of the story, these anecdotes are arranged around a central idea. Some topics lend themselves to this thematic focus rather than to the more traditional structure of the conflict/resolution plot design.

HOW TO TEACH IT

Most stories involve a series of events connected in time. These stories can easily be charted on a time line. But sometimes a writer will decide not to connect events in this way. Instead, the writer arranges a series of experiences that revolve around one theme. Cynthia Rylant does this in her book *When I Was Young in the Mountains*. If we were to map this story, it might look something like this:

Swimming in the water hole   Visiting the country store

Growing up
in the mountains

Baths in front of the woodstove

A story like this reminds me of a strand of pearls. It matters less how you order the pearls and more that they are all connected by the strand or focus you select. The challenge in this kind of text is to carefully select those moments that add up to the central feeling or idea you are trying to convey.

Does your story have anecdotal moments that are unconnected by a central time frame? If so, you may be working on a no-time narrative with a structure similar to one of the books I've mentioned. When you write this kind of story, consider whether you've selected the best moments to convey your main idea.

Pruning the Bushes—Cutting What You Don't Need

▲▲▲▲▲▲▲▲▲▲▲▲▲

RESOURCE MATERIAL

■ Story excerpts on clam digging (see Appendixes 17, 18, and 19)

▼▼▼▼▼▼▼▼▼▼▼▼▼

DISCUSSION

Learning to write succinctly is an important skill for writers. There is a saying: "I'm sorry I wrote you such a long letter. I would have written you a shorter one if I had more time." Lucy Calkins reminds us that a writer must be "passion hot, critic cold." The critic carefully rereads the writing and asks, Do I need this? If not, the unnecessary text should be cut. Students might be more willing to cut if we show them exactly how to do so. This craft lesson takes a bit longer than some others, but we consider it time well spent.

HOW TO TEACH IT

We had a big patch of raspberry bushes, but one year we didn't get a very good crop of berries. We decided to hire somebody to look at them. Two men came to the house with clipping shears and step ladders, and went to work. They cut so much off the bushes there was hardly anything left when they were finished. The men assured me that the bushes would be fine, and they were right. That spring we had our best crop ever.

Writing is another kind of plant that needs to be vigorously pruned if it's going to thrive. Here's the beginning of a story about clam digging. Let's take a minute and read it together.

(Read story excerpt from Appendix 17.)

This is a first draft. The author went back and asked himself, Are there any parts here that I don't need? Are there any parts where I'm getting off the topic? Are there any parts where the story gets bogged down?

Let me show you what he decided. Here's how he marked the text.

(Show piece with deletions, Appendix 18.)

Here's how the piece looks after the cuts have been made.

(Show Appendix 19.)

Cutting text can be a powerful tool, but it's not something you should be thinking about when you're just getting started. Let the writing flow, and don't censor yourself. Later, when you finish your first draft, go back and reread it. Ask yourself: Are there sections or sentences that I could cut? Are there places where I'm getting bogged down or drifting off my topic? You may be surprised to find how much better your writing sounds once you have cut the parts that bog it down.

Selecting the Right Lead

RESOURCE MATERIAL

■ Various leads (see Appendix 20)

DISCUSSION

Finding just the right lead to fit your writing takes time and attention. It also requires that students understand the range of options available. Some pieces of writing start slow and quiet; others startle the reader to attention with an odd fact or disturbing detail. We find that when students labor over the opening lines of their work, the energy of the lead can have an impact on the entire piece.

HOW TO TEACH IT

The lead can make or break your writing. When it works, the reader becomes a sympathetic and friendly audience, willing to listen to what you have to say. When it doesn't, the reader may stop and never go beyond the opening paragraph.

Writers use different kinds of leads, selecting the right one for the purpose at hand. Today I want to share several different kinds of leads.

(Show various leads.)

Let's all be on the lookout, not only for these leads but for other kinds as well. If one of these seems right, consider trying to write one for the piece you're working on.

Using Surprising Imagery

RESOURCE MATERIAL

■ *Parrot in the Oven: Mi Vida* by Victor Martinez

ALTERNATIVE TEXTS

■ *Holes* by Louis Sachar ("Stanley gazed out across the lake, toward the spot where he had been digging yesterday when he found the gold tube. He dug the hole into his memory" [71].)

■ *The Borning Room* by Paul Fleischman

DISCUSSION

Have you ever noticed how students play it safe with the description they include in their stories? Description becomes rich and vivid when writers compare two things most of us wouldn't think to put together. We can encourage students to be bold when writing description by showing them how other writers make this work.

HOW TO TEACH IT

A good story has lots of description tucked in and around the plot. This helps the reader enter the experience of the story. One way to write vivid description is to compare one thing to another. The best comparisons are often two things you wouldn't normally think of putting together. Consider Victor Martinez's description of cold wind:

> Anybody could see how cold it got. The wind already had glass edges to it, stiffening muscles and practically cutting through the stitches of our clothes. When it blew, the chill stabbed our teeth like icicles, and our voices jiggled every time we talked.

Martinez has taken one thing (wind) and compared it to another (glass). Notice how he moves beyond just saying it once. He extends the comparison by showing what wind would do if it really were like glass. It would cut through stitches of clothing; it would stab teeth like icicles.

Today when you read over your writing, find those places where you describe something. Could you make the description more vivid by comparing one thing to another thing? Be bold in your thinking.

Varying Length of Sentences

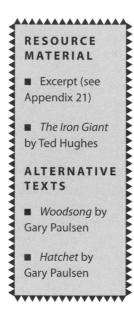

RESOURCE MATERIAL

■ Excerpt (see Appendix 21)

■ *The Iron Giant* by Ted Hughes

ALTERNATIVE TEXTS

■ *Woodsong* by Gary Paulsen

■ *Hatchet* by Gary Paulsen

DISCUSSION

Much of the writing we read has a numbing sameness to it. Often each sentence has the same rhythm, and roughly the same length, with an overall effect that dulls the reader's senses. When judiciously placed, a short sentence can pack a wallop. And it can give the writing contrast and texture.

HOW TO TEACH IT

When we write, we are trying to create an effect for the reader. You can do this by varying the length of the sentences. You might lull the reader into complacency with several rather long sentences and then—WHAM! a short sentence. Fragment. When used in the right way a short sentence or sentence fragment can have dramatic power.

(Read excerpt, Appendix 21.)

(You might also take a look at the first page of *The Iron Giant*, a book by the English poet Ted Hughes. The iron man falls off a cliff, and as he falls apart, the language falls apart and becomes fragmentary. As he begins to put himself together, the language does the same thing.)

Keep this in mind as you revisit the piece you're working on. As you reread, try to notice whether your sentences all have roughly the same length. If they do, you might want to follow several longer sentences with a very short one. This can be a potent tool in your writing. After you've done this, you'll want to read it over and see how it sounds.

The Recurring Line

RESOURCE MATERIAL

■ *Chicken Sunday* by Patricia Polacco

ALTERNATIVE TEXTS

■ *My Mama Had a Dancing Heart* by Libba Moore Gray

■ *Mrs. Katz and Tush* by Patricia Polacco

DISCUSSION

Some writers (poets as well as narrative writers) use a line or phrase that recurs throughout the text. A recurring line is like a rolling snowball—it gains power and weight as it gets repeated. Such a line can give cohesion to a piece and leave the reader with a sense of closure. Lynn Herschlein teaches fifth grade in Long Island, New York. Here's how she helps her students use this technique in their writing.

HOW TO TEACH IT

"Over the course of many read-alouds, we create a class chart of techniques used by our favorite authors," Lynn says. "One of the most concrete, accessible strategies for my students is the recurring line. Patricia Polacco uses it often. In *Chicken Sunday*, Miss Eula's voice is described as 'slow thunder and sweet rain.' This wonderful line appears three times in the story—at the beginning, toward the middle/end, and finally as an ending. When we read the book to examine the technique, my kids have already heard the story before—very important! When I come to the recurring line, they all say it aloud with me.

"Now my kids search their own work for a favorite line to use. Sometimes a peer points out a wonderful line. This line gets 'planted' in the writing, usually at the end and at various other places. Of course, other revisions are often necessary to make it work. Once a writer uses this technique successfully, I invite the student to share it with the class. This leads to many kids using the same technique.

"For many kids, the recurring line is a manageable way to provide closure. And it feels almost lyrical to them, I think. I like the results, especially seeing the thinking that goes on to come up with the right line or to make a particular one fit. Sometimes the writing comes out sounding a little forced, but mostly it works."

Craft Lessons: Teaching Writing K–8 **SECOND EDITION**

Writing Low on the "Food Chain"

RESOURCE MATERIAL

■ "Food chain" chart (see Appendix 22)

■ "Broken Chain" by Gary Soto

ALTERNATIVE TEXT

■ *Harry Potter and the Sorcerer's Stone* by J. K. Rowling. (Check out the beginning of the scene in Chapter 5, when Harry enters the wand shop in Diagon Alley for wonderful low-on-the-food-chain details describing the shop.)

DISCUSSION

As writing teachers we may wonder if our students listen to us at all. We make suggestions, give advice, but often find little evidence in their writing that they paid attention to our words. Perhaps we need to look at ourselves. We may have said certain things ("Show, don't tell") so many times the words have lost their meaning. Our challenge is to find fresh ways to express old but important ideas.

This craft lesson urges students to use more concrete details by writing low on the "food chain" of ideas. Students study the food chain in the ocean or land as a scientific concept; they can apply this understanding to the world of writing. Students should be familiar with the short story cited in the next section.

HOW TO TEACH IT

You've all studied the food chain in biology. In the ocean, one-celled bacteria get eaten by tiny plankton, which get eaten by small fish, which get eaten by larger fish, and so on. Well, in writing there is also a kind of food chain of ideas.

(Show "food chain" chart.)

The most general ideas live up here at the top of the food chain. They feed off the specific details that live lower on the food chain.

I want you to recall "Broken Chain," a story by Gary Soto. Remember that Alfonso didn't think he was very good-looking. Let's write that up here. But a general feeling like that has to be supported by specific details that a reader can picture. Do you remember the details Soto gives us? Alfonso does push-ups to make deep ripples in his stomach. And he's obsessed with the fact that his teeth are crooked, "like a pile of wrecked cars." There's that unforgettable detail of Alfonso spending hours trying to push his teeth straight with his thumb.

Often we tend to write too high on the food chain. In other words, we say too many general things ("He's helpful" or "She's wicked mean") without giving enough of the supporting details. The writer Donald Murray has said that "readers are bottom feeders." In other words, readers need the details in your writing. Make sure you have included enough gritty details to support the big ideas you want to get across. When you reread, you may realize you need to go back and add some.

Naming a Place or Character

RESOURCE MATERIAL

■ *What Jamie Saw* by Carolyn Coman

■ *Fig Pudding* by Ralph Fletcher

■ "My Stepfather, Rowdy" (see Appendix 7)

DISCUSSION

Name something and it starts to become real. It sounds so simple and obvious, but it's true. Don Graves explores this idea in his book *Experiment with Fiction* (1989). Our students can select names to breathe life into the places and characters they are writing about.

HOW TO TEACH IT

As a writer, you need to do whatever you can to help a story come alive in the mind of the reader. Here's a simple way of helping your setting or your characters come alive for the reader: name them!

I can write, "One day a kid walked home from school." So far I've got a nameless, faceless boy. I haven't given the reader much to go on. But look what happens when I write, "One afternoon Tommy Wallbanger stepped off the bus." All of a sudden I can feel my character begin to come alive.

Naming works for a place as well as a character. In Carolyn Coman's book *What Jamie Saw*, Jamie and his mother move to Stark, New Hampshire. The very name of this town—Stark—conveys the idea of a bleak, lifeless landscape in the middle of winter.

Sometimes the name you choose can communicate some idea of what the character or place is like. Certainly Maniac McGee gives the image of a certain kind of person. In the story "My Stepfather, Rowdy," the name Rowdy suggests a certain kind of person—playful, unpredictable, maybe a bit wild.

(*Note from Ralph Fletcher*: But names shouldn't be caricatures, either. I could have chosen fancy names for the kids in my book *Fig Pudding*, but I decided instead to use regular names: Cliff, Nate, Cyn (short for Cynthia), Teddy, Brad, Josh. I deliberately chose normal names in the spirit of a realistic novel about family life.)

Think about this today when you write. Do you have names for the people and places you're writing about? Do the names you've chosen fit the people and places you're writing about?

Remember: creating a believable character or setting doesn't happen automatically. You'll want to use description with compelling details. But naming the characters or the setting is a good way to start.

Describing a Character (1)

RESOURCE MATERIAL

■ *A Christmas Memory* by Truman Capote

■ "Raymond" by Paul Janeczko (see Appendix 23)

DISCUSSION

Our students need all the help we can give them to bring alive the characters they are writing about. Mike McCormick, a sixth-grade teacher in Alaska, helps his students use telling details to describe their characters.

HOW TO TEACH IT

"I have my best success when I confer with a student who is writing at the beginning of a rough-draft stage," Mike says. "I dig up relevant literature and give it to that student to read. Then I have a conference with the student about that piece of literature (sometimes I read it out loud to the student) before the student goes back to his or her writing.

"For instance, my students often want to write about their friends or members of their family. Here's what I do:

1. I might read aloud a section from *A Christmas Memory* by Truman Capote. There's a wonderful part where Truman and his aunt are standing in the kitchen.
2. I might suggest to my students, 'Write a scene in which you show you and your friend together. The scene should describe how you both look, the place you're in.'
3. I'll read aloud the Capote excerpt one more time so the students can focus in on how he did it.
4. I send the kids off to write.

"In a variation of this, I use 'Raymond,' a poem by Paul Janeczko in *Brickyard Summer*. I read the poem, then I ask students to jot down a description of the friend they want to write about, and a couple of things they did with that friend. I ask them to tell somewhere in the piece how long they've been friends."

Describing a Character (2)

RESOURCE MATERIAL

■ Excerpt from
Yolonda's Genius
by Carol Fenner
(see Appendix 24)

ALTERNATIVE TEXT

■ Excerpt from
*Harry Potter and
the Sorcerer's Stone*
by J. K. Rowling
(see Appendix 24)

DISCUSSION

An important way to create character is through physical description. Skilled writers know how to do this without providing static portraits. They select details that draw on the reader's five senses, and they use these descriptions in the context of the character's actions.

These written interludes often occur outside of the plot line of the story. You might encourage your writers to generate descriptions separate from the story line and then to place them in the text as needed.

HOW TO TEACH IT

Today we're going to talk about the way writers create physical descriptions of their characters to paint a clear picture in the reader's mind.

Listen as I read aloud the following passage from *Yolonda's Genius* by Carol Fenner. Pay attention to the image these details conjure in your mind.

(Read.)

Notice how Fenner appeals to all of our senses in providing this portrait of Aunt Tiny. She invites us to hear her laugh, see her bright clothes, smell and taste her cooking, and feel the warmth of her "big, soft hug." These selected details allow us to fill in the rest of the picture. We know from this description that Aunt Tiny is warm, friendly, and feminine. Yolonda loves her. The author doesn't tell us any of this directly, but we know it because we have a living, moving picture of Aunt Tiny in our minds.

When you return to your writing today, I want you to reread and look for places where you physically describe your characters. If you haven't done that yet, you might try writing descriptions that draw on more than a visual picture. You could write these descriptions in your notebook or on a sheet separate from your story. You can worry later about where they best fit. For now, try to conjure an image of your character and put it in writing.

Here's one tip: describe your character doing something. It might not make sense to describe your character cooking, as Fenner described Aunt Tiny. So think: What would make sense for your character to be doing? Would it help readers to see her stuffing her locker at school, rummaging through her closet for an outfit for a party, waiting impatiently for friends to arrive for a sleepover? Be bold!

Describing a Character Through Gesture

RESOURCE MATERIAL

■ *The Watsons Go to Birmingham— 1963* by Christopher Paul Curtis

ALTERNATIVE TEXT

■ *Flying Solo* by Ralph Fletcher (excerpt, page 26: "Christopher Ransom lumbered into the room. 'I'm ready to go home now!' he announced, flopping down onto his desk and stretching out two big feet.")

DISCUSSION

Young writers typically pay more attention to the plot than the characters. Writing teachers can help sensitize students to the issue of characterization, but when we raise this issue we have to be able to provide them with specific, practical strategies. Gesture is a powerful tool for a writer, but students rarely use it. We suggest you model this strategy using a book students are familiar with.

HOW TO TEACH IT

When a certain kindergarten girl feels shy, she takes a piece of her hair, puts it into her mouth, and begins to chew. Another student in her class, a boy, shows his excitement by reaching up and pulling down, hard, on an imaginary rope as he cries: "Yesssss!!!!"

These are all gestures—physical motions made by people. Describing a particular gesture is one of the best ways to bring alive a character.

Physical gestures—a sarcastic bow, a toss of the hair, a crinkling up of the nose—give the reader a way to visualize your character. And since a gesture usually reflects an emotional state, it gives us an excellent way to reveal what a character is feeling at a particular time.

When a four-year-old boy gets frustrated, he throws back his head. A woman sighs and chews her upper lip. A man briskly rubs his face. Three characters feeling the same thing (frustration) will have three different gestures to show it.

Christopher Paul Curtis uses gesture to develop the mother's character in his novel *The Watsons Go to Birmingham—1963*. The book is narrated by a boy named Kenny, who describes the mother making this gesture: "Momma put her hand over her mouth. She did this whenever she was going to smile because she had a great big gap between her front teeth."

At the end of the novel, a bomb explodes in a church in Birmingham, Alabama. At first, the mother fears that her daughter was in the church when it got bombed. Now Kenny returns to that gesture: "Momma was so upset that she even forgot to cover the space in her front teeth."

Think about your characters as you reread your writing. Will your readers be able to picture them? Have you described them doing something? Even a small gesture will go a long way toward making the character come alive on the page.

Getting Your Characters Talking

RESOURCE MATERIAL

■ Large chart

■ *The Tiger Rising* by Kate DiCamillo

ALTERNATIVE TEXTS

■ *Olive's Ocean* by Kevin Henkes pp. 38–41. Five different characters (mom, dad, grandma, toddler, and Martha) speak in this scene, and you get a sense of each personality as they do so.

■ *Mississippi Bridge* by Mildred Taylor pp. 17–18. You can hear the prejudice in the voice of Mr. Wallace and the subservience in the voice of Josias.

DISCUSSION

Just as a picture can be worth a thousand words, a few words of well-crafted dialogue can paint a clearer picture of any character. Some kids will start using dialogue naturally; others will need a nudge.

HOW TO TEACH IT

When you write a story, you want to do all you can to show readers how your characters act, think, and feel. A good way to do this is by writing dialogue—by having them talk to each other. Listen to this excerpt from *The Tiger Rising* by Kate DiCamillo.

(Read from pages 22 to 25.)

Let's talk about what the dialogue reveals about each of the characters.

(Draw a line down the middle of a chart. On one side of the line note something you learn about Sistine or Rob. On the other side, note the specific lines of dialogue that show this. Kids might note that Sistine is a little toughy but also smart and shy. You can sense Rob's timidness. Talk about what the dialogue tells you about the characters and about their relationship.)

We learn all of this just by listening to the characters talk. If you haven't used dialogue in the story you are working on, look for a place where you could get your characters talking. When you write this dialogue, think about each character's personality and the specific way they would speak. Write a few lines back and forth, and then stop and reread. Ask yourself: is this the way this person would sound?

One caution: don't overuse dialogue. The trick is to select just enough detail to reveal your characters.

Using Interior Monologue

RESOURCE MATERIAL

■ Story excerpt (see Appendix 25)

DISCUSSION

It's so hard for young writers to create characters who come alive on the page. Typically we learn far more about what's going on outside the characters than we do about what's going on inside them. Interior monologue requires young writers to imagine a character's inner life and re-create it for the reader.

HOW TO TEACH IT

Sometimes in a poem or story a character silently speaks without saying any actual words. This is called interior monologue, and it's an excellent way to give readers a window into a character's inner thoughts, emotions, and conflicts.

Interior monologue can take several forms. Sometimes the character addresses the reader in a short speech. Other times it's closer to an interior dialogue in which different parts of the same character talk (or even argue) back and forth, showing the reader different sides of him or herself.

In the following story excerpt you can get a feel for what an interior monologue might sound like.

(Read excerpt, Appendix 25.)

I want you to consider writing an interior monologue in the story you're working on. Take the most important character at a crucial moment, and get that character silently talking, using language that's most natural to him or her. Even a short interior monologue can help readers enter into the inner life of a character.

Copyright © 2007

Ralph Fletcher and

JoAnn Portalupi.

Stenhouse Publishers

Internal Conflict

RESOURCE MATERIAL

■ *Flying Solo* by Ralph Fletcher

ALTERNATIVE TEXT

■ *The Other Side* by Jacqueline Woodson

DISCUSSION

You can pull examples of internal conflict from familiar books and then encourage students to explore the internal conflicts of their own characters.

HOW TO TEACH IT

Sometimes the conflict in a story can be found inside a particular character. Think about the novel *Flying Solo*. In that book Bastian is moving to Hawaii and has just found out that his puppy will have to be quarantined for four months in Honolulu. This bothers Bastian terribly. At a crucial moment in the book, he has an important realization.

> "That's the kind of dog I want," Sean said. "I'm saving my money."
>
> "Yeah," Bastian said. And he felt it again. A rush of sadness—strange, mysterious—welling up inside him. And all at once he got it. He understood. He had been moving toward it all day, but he hadn't figured it out until that very moment.
>
> The sadness was about Barkley.
>
> Dad was right. It would be flat out wrong to put Barkley through the Quarantine. Four months was a hundred twenty-three days. Two thousand nine hundred and fifty-two hours. One hundred and seventy-seven thousand one hundred and twenty minutes. That was too long for a little puppy to wait, no matter how many times Bastian visited him. It would be cruel to put Barkley through all that.
>
> A moral decision. And he knew the right thing to do.
>
> He had to give Barkley away.
>
> Give Barkley away?!
>
> Yes.
>
> No decision had ever felt more right. Or made him feel more miserable.
>
> Now he understood the real reason for this rock ritual. It was a closure ritual. A chance to say good-bye, not to the other kids, but to Barkley. He tried out the words, saying them under his breath.
>
> Goodbye, Barkley.

You might want to describe an internal conflict in your own writing. This requires you to go inside the character's psychology, to give us a window on the thinking involved as that character weighs the pros and cons of a difficult decision. An internal conflict will give your writing depth. And it will give the reader a chance to care about the fate of the character.

Adding Setting to a Story

RESOURCE MATERIAL

■ Excerpt from *A Sense of Where You Are* by John McPhee

DISCUSSION

Mike McCormick teaches sixth grade in Eagle River, Alaska. His thoughts about teaching young writers: "Writing teachers must constantly search out writing that connects with students' lives. The best teacher of writing is writing. Students must read pieces by writers who grappled with similar struggles, who adventured in similar environments, who found joy in similar activities. Just as musicians listen to tons of music, and artists study paintings and sculpture, so must writers study the work that has come before. Students should read the best writing available on a topic; often that is not children's writing but writing for adults."

Mike notices that students often write about their topics in a general way. They need strategies for making their writing more immediate, for digging beneath the surface. Here's how he helps his students bring alive their writing by creating a dramatic scene with a realistic setting.

HOW TO TEACH IT

"Let's say a student is writing about basketball in a very general way," Mike says. "I grab McPhee's *A Sense of Where You Are*, a book about Bill Bradley. I have the kid read the description of Princeton's gym where Bradley played":

> The basketball locker room in the gymnasium at Princeton has no blackboard, no water fountain, and, in fact, no lockers. Up on the main floor, things go along in the same vein. Collapsible grandstands pull out of the walls and crowd up to the edge of the court. Jolly alumni sometimes wander in just before a game begins, sit down on the players' bench, and are permitted to stay there. The players themselves are a little slow getting started each year, because if they try to do some practicing on their own during the autumn they find the gymnasium full of graduate students who know their rights and won't move over. When a fellow does get some action, it can be dangerous. The gym is so poorly designed that a scrimmage player can be knocked down one of two flights of concrete stairs.

"Then I ask the student to write a description of the place where he plays. Suddenly the piece gets concrete—it gains a specific setting."

Setting to Reveal Character

RESOURCE MATERIAL

■ *Freak the Mighty* by Rodman Philbrick

■ *What Jamie Saw* by Carolyn Coman

ALTERNATIVE TEXT

■ *Holes* by Louis Sachar (Chapter 9 opens with a description of the shower and the "Wreck Room" at Camp Green Lake, which creates a context for the introduction of the boys who live there.)

DISCUSSION

The setting is more than backdrop: it can be an integral part of the writing that permeates the plot, creates tension, even develops the characters. This craft lesson draws on two fine young-adult novels to show writers of this age a sophisticated way for using the setting to deepen their writing.

HOW TO TEACH IT

Imagine a movie about a young woman whose beloved has left her. We see her staring out a rain-streaked window, wiping away her tears. This is no accident. The director chose this particular setting to reinforce the woman's emotional state.

Writers do the same thing. Sometimes a writer deliberately uses the setting to help bring alive the inner life of a character. Think of Max, the giant in *Freak the Mighty*. Max's huge size and slow brain have made him the butt of jokes. As the book begins, Max spends most of his time in his grandparents' basement, a place he calls the "down and under." It makes sense that this "dim hole in the ground" would be the only place a misfit like Max would feel comfortable. It's a place to hide.

You see the same thing in *What Jamie Saw*. Jamie, his mother, and the baby leave their house to get away from Van, the mother's boyfriend. They move to a tiny silver trailer. ("Jamie felt that he was in a box, or a hollowed-out bullet.") The author makes use of the setting outside the trailer in the same way. The landscape Jamie sees outside is as cold and frozen as the feelings inside him.

Think of the setting when you write. You can describe a setting that will give readers a hint as to what is going on inside the main characters. Even if you can't change the setting you're writing about, you might choose to describe particular weather, or a specific time of day, to create a particular mood that will reflect a character's inner life.

Setting That Shapes the Action

RESOURCE MATERIAL

■ *Phoenix Rising* by Karen Hesse

■ *Out of the Dust* by Karen Hesse

ALTERNATIVE TEXTS

■ *The House of the Scorpion* by Nancy Farmer

■ *The One O'Clock Chop* by Ralph Fletcher

DISCUSSION

Young writers don't pay much attention to setting. Much maligned, mostly ignored, the setting remains pretty limp in most student writing. We can show kids how sensory details can bring setting alive, but that doesn't go far enough. Even after a writer enhances the setting, the place often remains in the background, with no real connection to the action of the piece.

The two novels cited in this lesson can also be used as examples of the person versus nature conflict.

HOW TO TEACH IT

We've been talking about the sense of place in writing. Today we're going to look at how the setting can be an integral part of the story and actually shape what happens.

Karen Hesse is one writer who knows the power of the setting in her books. In *Phoenix Rising* the setting has an enormous impact on the plot as well as on the characters. This novel takes place on a Vermont sheep farm. There has been a recent explosion at a nearby nuclear plant. Many of the people and farm animals in the area have been poisoned by radiation.

The setting in this book is hostile and ominous, and Hesse uses vivid details to bring it alive. The very first scene shows Nyle Sumner, the main character, walking on her grandmother's farm. Nyle is wearing a gauze mask, and we learn that she has had to wear it for the past week. Soon Nyle and her family have to take in a boy who has been severely poisoned by radiation.

(*Out of the Dust*, also by Karen Hesse, gives many striking examples of characters whose lives are molded by the harsh conditions of the Dust Bowl.)

I want you to reread your writing. Ask yourself, Have I used details that really describe the place where my story happens? How might my setting become more central to my story? How might it affect what happens?

Slowing Down the "Hot Spot"

RESOURCE MATERIAL

■ *Fig Pudding* by Ralph Fletcher

ALTERNATIVE TEXTS

■ *Shiloh* by Phyllis Reynolds Naylor

■ *Homesick, My Own Story* by Jean Fritz

DISCUSSION

Our students tend to be extremely democratic when they write: each part of the story gets equal attention. A detail from the beginning often gets the same amount of space as a crucial incident near the end. It's not uncommon for students to skim quickly over the climactic moments of their narratives. We can help them sift through their writing and figure out which parts are most important. Once they know this, we can help them slow down the "hot spot," or climax. This craft lesson assumes that students are familiar with *Fig Pudding*.

HOW TO TEACH IT

A good piece of writing will often build up to a hot spot, or climax. Think back on "The Tackle Box" chapter in *Fig Pudding*. Remember that Cliff didn't want his little brothers and sisters to use his tackle box. So he took all the fishing gear out and stuffed in rags, diapers, underwear, to make the tackle box feel heavy. The next day Cliff watched as his father packed up the car to take the other kids fishing.

(Read this scene on page 63 of the paperback version of *Fig Pudding*.)

This is a definite hot spot in the story. It's a crucial moment in the writing, a point of suspense and high emotion. You don't want to rush through the hot spot when you write. In fact, this is one part that authors usually try to slow down.

Moviemakers often use slow motion to dramatize the hot spots in films. Writers have to use words to slow down the action. In the excerpt we just read, the hot spot gets slowed down in three ways:

1. Talking: dialogue makes us feel like we're in the midst of the scene.
2. Showing frame-by-frame detail: the crushed-gravel driveway, the car window opening, Dad's "short, hard look."
3. Going inside a character: "I was already dead, my heart not beating, lungs not working, legs frozen to the ground."

Think about your own writing. Do you have a hot spot in your story? If not, maybe you need to build up to a moment of suspense and tension. If you do have a hot spot, make sure you haven't rushed through this part of your story. You can slow down a hot spot by using dialogue, detail, and a peek inside the character you're writing about.

Using Flashback

DISCUSSION

Once students learn how to use flashback they are freed from writing a story in a straightforward, linear fashion. These glimpses into the past can be used to develop character, invite readers into significant moments gone by, or make contrasts that point to important changes that have occurred.

HOW TO TEACH IT

Today I want to talk about the flashback. Sometimes a writer is moving along in a story and wants to show the reader something that happened in the past. Directors use this in films as well. Think of it as a cut from the action where the director signals to the viewer that you are going to view something that happened at another time. A well-placed flashback can enrich the present scene you are watching. Writers use this technique, too.

Patricia MacLachlan uses a flashback in her book *Sarah, Plain and Tall*. The story begins with the scene of Caleb talking with his sister Anna about the day he was born—and the day their mother died. Anna is kneading dough while Caleb is sitting in front of the fire. MacLachlan uses Anna's daydreaming to flash back to the scene of her mother's funeral.

> I looked at the long dirt road that crawled across the plains, remembering the morning that Mama had died, cruel and sunny. They had come for her in a wagon and taken her away.

This flashback takes us back to a significant moment in Anna's past. Knowing about this past event allows us to experience more fully Anna's present situation.

Think about your story. Is there a past event in the life of a character you want the reader to know about? Is there some scene you might allow us to view through the use of a flashback? I'm hoping some of you will experiment with this. We'll make time over the next few days to listen to and talk about the flashbacks you create.

Flashback/Time Transitions

RESOURCE MATERIAL

■ Large chart

■ *Yolonda's Genius* by Carol Fenner

■ *Wringer* by Jerry Spinelli

■ *Belle Prater's Boy* by Ruth White

DISCUSSION

It's easier to recognize when a writer employs a particular technique than it is to use it in your own writing. Students may be able to identify flashback when they read it in other people's books but stumble in trying to embed it in their own writing. We can help students by getting specific about the language writers use to make these time transitions.

HOW TO TEACH IT

We've been talking about flashback in writing. Today let's continue by taking a closer look at the specific ways writers make the transition from one point of time to another.

(On a large chart write out the following examples [or ones you find in your own favorite books]. Discuss how the sentences signal to the reader that a flashback follows.)

Once, when we were about ten, I saw Woodrow . . . (*Belle Prater's Boy*, p. 8)

Her mind traveled. Images from long ago slipped slow-motion through her head. (*Yolonda's Genius*, p. 38)

Palmer tried to hold the moment there, but it would not stay. It tunneled back through time and burst up onto this same field three years before, the first Saturday in August, when the grass was streaked with red and guns were booming and birds were falling. (*Wringer*, p. 17)

You can use a very simple transition (e.g., "I remember when," "Once long ago"), or you can write a more complex one, just as Spinelli did in *Wringer*. Have fun and experiment. Let's add to this list by collecting the time transitions you invent for your own writing.

Using a Transition Sentence

RESOURCE MATERIAL

■ "Moving Madness" (Appendix 26)

ALTERNATIVE TEXT

■ "Other Examples of Transition Sentences" (Appendix 27)

DISCUSSION

Transition is a simple word but a difficult skill. High school students, college students, even adults struggle to write smooth transitions. We introduce this idea knowing it will be a real stretch for many young writers. Even so, it's worth making students aware of this concept through a model, and inviting them to try it in their writing.

HOW TO TEACH IT

A transition is a movement or passage from one idea, or time, to another. You don't want to jerk your readers from one idea to the next. A transition sentence will help the change go more smoothly.

Let's read "Moving Madness." See if you can pick out the transition sentences.

(Discuss.)

You can see that at the end of the second paragraph, the author uses the word *forever*. That word gets used again: "But forever didn't last." That's a transition sentence. Let's see how this would sound without that transition sentence.

(Reread the first three paragraphs.)

It's much bumpier, much more abrupt, without the transition sentence. That sentence smoothes the passage from one idea (the perfect house) to the shocking news (Mom's new job in North Carolina). There's another transition sentence farther down. In one paragraph the writer tells about all the things he did that summer, but now he wants to move to the very last day. He uses a transition sentence to make that switch. You can see that the writer borrows a word from the previous sentence—*tomorrow*—and uses it in the transition sentence.

Keep a lookout for transition sentences you find in books you're reading. And start thinking of how you can use a transition in your writing to make a smooth change from one idea to the next. The first step is to locate a place where you are switching ideas, or jumping from one time to another. After you identify that place, see if you can write a sentence that helps the reader make a smooth transition.

Writing Through a Mask

RESOURCE MATERIAL

■ *Up North at the Cabin* by Marsha Wilson Chall

ALTERNATIVE TEXTS

■ "Song of the Dolphin" by Georgia Heard

■ *Sierra* by Diane Siebert

DISCUSSION

Poet Georgia Heard describes writing through a mask as one way to explore familiar subject matter in surprising, fresh ways. This craft lesson draws on a picture book short enough that students can read it quickly and grasp the author's technique.

HOW TO TEACH IT

We've read and enjoyed *Up North at the Cabin* and talked about how that book reminds us of special places each of us visit outside of our daily lives. Chall does something very specific to help us experience the place the way the girl in the story does. She uses a strategy called writing through a mask. The writer puts on a mask and then looks at the world as if she were the kind of person (or thing) the mask represents. Here is a list of the masks Chall wears as she narrates this story:

A smart angler
A gray dolphin
An acrobat
A fearless voyager
A daredevil

As I read this story, listen to what she does in the writing each time she puts on a mask.
(Read *Up North at the Cabin.*)
Writing through a mask can help you find fresh ways to write about a familiar subject. You might want to explore your topic by trying various masks. You can let your reader know what you are doing in the same way Chall does by telling us, "I am a great gray dolphin" or "I am an acrobat." Or you can keep the mask invisible and just use some of the descriptions the mask helped you to discover.

Experimenting with Irony

RESOURCE MATERIAL

■ "Another Night" (see Appendix 28)

ALTERNATIVE TEXTS

■ *Arlene Sardine* by Chris Raschka offers irony in a picture-book format.

■ "Passing" by Langston Hughes

DISCUSSION

Irony is a fascinating and potent literary device. True, it may lie beyond the reach of many writers in this age group, but we can teach it in the spirit of fun and experimentation. Students can try irony in their fiction, poetry, and nonfiction writing.

HOW TO TEACH IT

Irony is a special technique in writing. Writers who use irony create tension by stating one thing but meaning the opposite.

We often do this when we speak. A friend invites us for dinner and serves leftover tuna casserole, and we crack sarcastically, "This is the most delectable dinner I've ever had."

Irony is similar to sarcasm, but it's not exactly the same thing. Let's look at this poem, "Another Night." The poem depicts a boy and his mother watching Father come home at midnight, drunk. They rush to bed, "pretending to be asleep." Here's the last stanza:

Sun rises at dawn.
Good morning, Nebraska.
We're a perfect
farm family.

This is a good example of irony: the author states one thing, but we know that he means the opposite. This family is anything but perfect.

Irony is a powerful tool you can use in your own writing. Read over your writing. Do any of your sentences have any hidden meanings, or are they all straightforward and obvious? Irony is a good way to put a little edge into your writing, to make your sentences richer and more complex. You can experiment with irony in the beginning, middle, or end of the writing.

Experimenting with Symbolism

RESOURCE MATERIAL

■ *My Great-Aunt Arizona* by Gloria Houston

ALTERNATIVE TEXT

■ *The Other Side* by Jacqueline Woodson (the wooden fence)

DISCUSSION

Symbolism usually gets presented as one of the most serious, almost sacred literary techniques. The fact that students usually don't get introduced to it until high school or college literature courses would seem to put it beyond the reach of young writers.

But not so fast. We believe that many students are hungry for bigger writing challenges. Symbolism might be a good place to start. Remember that symbolism has turned students off literature because of the arbitrary way it often gets taught: In *Lord of the Flies*, the conch shell symbolizes civilization, which gets shattered when the conch shell gets broken. Tom Romano says, "Many 'good' literature students have been contaminated by the notion of symbolism, feeling that there were hidden meanings in everything, meanings they could never get. *Symbolism is something to explore, not get right*." When we share examples of symbolism with students, we need to give them plenty of room to make their own interpretations.

Teaching kids how to use symbolism in their writing begins with showing them how it is used in literature. You can draw examples of symbolism from picture books, poems, and novels. It's important to use familiar texts. As with any new technique, don't expect perfection when kids try to use it in their writing. It's important to value the attempt as much as the final product.

HOW TO TEACH IT

Today we're going to talk about symbolism in writing. Symbols are concrete objects or things that suggest or stand for something else.

My Great-Aunt Arizona, by Gloria Houston, is a portrait of a wonderful teacher. Aunt Arizona loves teaching, and she loves her students. With each class she teaches, she plants a fir tree outside the school. Over time the trees begin to tower over the little woman.

Why do you think Houston included these trees in the book? What might they mean? When I read this book, the trees make me think of all the students Aunt Arizona has taught. To me, they are visual reminders of all her students.

I'll be interested in hearing of other symbols you find in books you read.

You might experiment with symbolism in one of your own poems or stories. If you include a symbol, try to make it visual and concrete.

The Circular Ending

RESOURCE MATERIAL

■ *Smoky Night* by Eve Bunting

ALTERNATIVE TEXTS

■ *Tuck Everlasting* by Natalie Babbitt

■ *The Trip Back Home* by Janet S. Wong

DISCUSSION

The circular ending is a winner. It's easy to teach and easy for students to grasp, and they'll have fun trying it out in their own writing. A circular ending gives the reader a satisfying feeling of completion and wholeness. As a writing strategy, the circular ending is related to the recurring line (discussed in a previous lesson). After students are familiar with *Smoky Night*, you can take them into a deeper discussion of this book. To understand the circular ending, students have to look at the structure or architecture of the book.

HOW TO TEACH IT

Today we're going to talk about using a circular ending in writing. I want you to think about a book we read earlier this year, *Smoky Night*. In the opening scene the narrator holds his cat, Jasmine, safely in his arms. There's a lot of action after that—fire and turmoil—but the story closes with a boy stroking another cat.

(If your students know the book, you may want to mention *Tuck Everlasting*, a novel that models this kind of ending. The opening scene, in which Winnie watches the frog, recurs at the end of the novel.)

You may want to try a circular ending in your own writing. You might start with a favorite detail or reference and return to it at the very end. Or you may want to write it backward, in other words, you may want to first write the ending (for example the cat purring in Mrs. Kim's arms) and then find a way to insert a reference to this detail earlier in the book.

Selecting Livelier Adjectives

▲▲▲▲▲▲▲▲▲▲▲▲▲▲

**RESOURCE
MATERIAL**

■ Excerpt from
"Barry Bonds's
Enhancements" by
George F. Will
(Appendix 29)

▼▼▼▼▼▼▼▼▼▼▼▼▼▼

DISCUSSION

Adjectives in writing are like salt in cooking—a little goes a long way. Many people tend to over-salt dishes. And many novice writers tend to overuse adjectives.

Ben Yagoda wrote a book titled *If You Catch an Adjective, Kill It.* We wouldn't go that far. The goal of this lesson is to sensitize students to this issue, and suggest that less is better.

HOW TO TEACH IT

An adjective is a part of speech that describes a noun or a pronoun. This makes the meaning of the noun more specific. For example: the *warm* rain. His *enormous* hands.

Listen to this sentence: *At noon the tired, muddy, defeated, sweaty army finally stopped for a timely and well-deserved break.*

Is this good writing? (Discuss.)

The sentence I just read contains many adjectives—too many. It's overwritten. In fact you don't need to use a long list of adjectives to write a strong descriptive sentence. Rather, you should select one or two, but make sure the adjectives you select are lively ones.

Let's look at the beginning of an essay about Barry Bonds written by George F. Will. As you read it, pay close attention to the adjectives this writer uses. Underline them.

(Share copies of "Barry Bonds's Enhancements" Appendix 29.)

What adjectives did you find? Which ones did you admire? Why? (Discuss.)

In the second sentence the author describes Bonds making a "long trudge toward tainted glory." The adjective "tainted" colors the noun, and makes us understand that he means glory in a particular way.

Today as you write, see if you can incorporate adjectives that are livelier and more interesting to read.

Using Hyphenated Descriptive Words

RESOURCE MATERIAL

■ Paragraph copied on individual sheets or printed on a large chart

DISCUSSION

Middle school writers are ready for more sophisticated strategies that kick their writing up to the next level. Here is a nifty technique for creating descriptive writing that sounds fresh and interesting. This lesson can piggyback on the lesson that precedes this one, "Selecting Livelier Adjectives."

HOW TO TEACH IT

If you're like most people, you go through periods where your sentences have a serious case of the blahs. They don't contain errors, exactly, but they're just not very exciting to read. Using more interesting adjectives is one way you can rejuvenate a dull sentence.

Let's take a look at this paragraph. As we read it together, I want you to pay particular attention to the adjectives used to describe the nouns.

(Make the following paragraph large enough to be visible.)

It had been a terrific beach day. It was hot, but the cloud-studded sky gave just enough shade to keep things tolerable. When the storm hit, it seemed to catch the sun-drugged tourists by surprise. As the rain pounded down, you could see them frantically gathering clothes and baskets and beach toys. They ran toward the parking lot, leaving a soaked, litter-strewn beach in their wake.

Did you notice anything interesting or unusual about the adjectives you found?

(Discuss.)

This piece includes several hyphenated words: cloud-studded, sun-drugged. Using two words linked together by a hyphen is an excellent way a writer can create an adjective that is fresh and unique.

Take a closer look at this kind of a hyphenated adjective, the *rain-drenched streets*, for example. Note that this kind of adjective usually consists of a noun (rain) followed by the verb (drenched). Today when you write, I invite you to experiment with this technique. I'll be curious to see if anyone uses a hyphenated adjective in your writing.

Refining Your Title

RESOURCE MATERIAL

■ Your own or student writing

Some of our favorite titles:

■ *Wilma Unlimited* by Kathleen Krull

■ *Dancing on the Edge* by Han Nolan

■ *Smoky Night* by Eve Bunting

DISCUSSION

Titles serve at least two purposes during the process of draft to finished piece. When a student first places a title on the top of an empty page, the title is serving the writer's need. It points a direction; it helps jump-start the writing to come. But, too often, this initial title never gets reconsidered. The title serves a different purpose in the final draft. Now its job is to serve the reader, to extend an invitation to enter into the piece of writing.

HOW TO TEACH IT

Today I want to talk about the title as a doorway to a piece of writing. I notice that many of you find it helpful to begin your writing by choosing a title. Often this title names your topic. I do this, too. For instance, I have a story about the time my eldest son lost one of his last baby teeth. I chose a working title of "Taylor's Tooth." This title was a doorway I entered to get into the story. It helped me begin to write.

Now that I have finished writing, I can see that my story has changed somewhat. Now my story is more about my son's saying goodbye to being a child than it is about losing a single tooth. As I finish my story I have to think about the title, not as a way for me to get started, but as something for the reader. I know that the title on my finished piece will be the door the reader steps through to get into the story. Here are two new titles I'm considering:

Saying Goodbye
Last Visit from the Tooth Fairy

Some of you are working on the final touches of a piece of writing. If so, take a minute to think about whether you've written a title that invites the reader in. You don't always want to give away the story by naming the topic. Brainstorm a few different titles and run them by a reader. Reconsidering your title is a good way to clarify for yourself what is most important about your topic.

Beware Formulaic Writing

RESOURCE MATERIAL

■ "Benefits of the Computer" (Appendixes 30 and 31)

DISCUSSION

Formulaic writing is one of the by-products of the test mania that has infected so many school districts across the country. Some teachers might argue that the exemplar used in this lesson is adequate; we believe that students should reach for something better.

HOW TO TEACH IT

Have you ever seen one of those paint-by-numbers art kits that promise to turn you into an artist? You get paint and brushes. You get the outline of the painting with lots of little numbers to tell you which color you should paint, and exactly where you should paint them.

You have been learning how to write a good story, or poem, or essay. But if you're not careful—if you're *too* careful—your writing can end up looking like one of those paint-by-numbers paintings. It can seem bland and lifeless.

Let's take a close look at a short essay, "Benefits of the Computer." Please follow along as I read this out loud.

(Pass out copies of the first version from Appendix 30 to students, or enlarge so all can see.)

What did you think about this essay?

(Discuss.)

This is a five-paragraph essay. In some ways, the writing isn't bad. It has three main points divided into three paragraphs. Each paragraph begins with a topic sentence. On a five-point scale it's probably a three. But the writing feels "canned," as if the writer is following a formula. The introduction tells you what it's going to tell you; the conclusion repeats what the writer has already told you. It's very predictable. There's not much life in this essay. We don't hear the author's voice coming through.

Now let's look at how you could write about the same topic in a different way.

(Share second version from Appendix 31.)

How did this one differ from the first one we read?

(Discuss.)

Beware formulaic writing. You should be aware of the guidelines we have talked about, but at the same time remember that none of them are rigid rules etched in stone. Don't be afraid to use a flourish—a lively verb, surprising fragment, amazing fact, a question, or even some sly humor—to make your writing sound like you and come alive.

Questions and Answers

*H*ow has your thinking on teaching the writer's craft evolved since Craft Lessons *was first published?*

Craft Lessons looks at an assortment of craft elements: leads, endings, verbs, time, characterization, setting, and so forth. One big development occurred when we started working on a curriculum resource, *Teaching the Qualities of Writing* (2004). We began to wonder if all these craft elements might fit into larger clusters. We decided that in fact the various craft elements do fall naturally into four categories we called the "qualities of writing":

Ideas: The writer must have something to say. Strong writing conveys rich, plentiful ideas that are developed in engaging, even surprising ways.

Design: In the hands of a skillful writer, ideas are presented in an orderly fashion. Strong writing has shape, architecture, and overall design.

Language: The language a writer chooses directly affects how we experience the ideas found on the page. In a strong piece of writing, the language allows ideas to take flight.

Presentation: Every possible barrier that stands between the writer and the reader—messy handwriting, incorrect spelling, and disorderly papers—has to be removed. Successful writing respects the reader's need for clean, correct presentation.

Teachers familiar with *Teaching the Qualities of Writing* may find it useful to incorporate the craft lessons in this book into TQW, or vice versa. To facilitate that, we provide a list of the craft lessons in this book divided by Ideas, Design, and Language in the "Qualities of Writing Index." (There are no Presentation lessons.)

There's something missing in this book. Where are the craft lessons on para-graphing, noun-verb agreement, fragments, and run-ons?

A book like this one can only accomplish so much. We make a distinction between teaching the elements of good writing (craft) and the grammar of writing (mechanics). True, this distinction is somewhat arbitrary; at times the two are interconnected. But for the purposes of this book we made a decision to focus on issues of craft. The skills you mention are extremely important, but we didn't believe we could do justice to them in this partic-ular book.

These lessons sound great but some of them don't sound like me. When I read certain craft lessons I realize I might teach it differently from what you say in the "How to Teach It" section. Suggestions?

Don't let this book turn you away from your own experience as a reader, writer, and teacher. It's important to remember that all the craft lessons in this book have fingerprints on them, the fingerprints of a living, breathing person. The lessons contributed by teachers have been shaped by their own particular ways of reading, and by the students they have shared them with. Our lessons also reflect each of our experiences and unique ways of seeing texts.

For these lessons to come alive you need to find ways to make them your own. Be on the lookout for ways to personalize them. For example, we might suggest a book to illustrate a craft lesson, but you may think of a different book to illustrate the point, a book your class already knows and loves. The lesson can proceed just as easily with your selection.

How do I start using this book? How do I decide which craft elements to begin with?

Naturally, there are lots of ways to approach this. We all have different tastes when it comes to the writer's craft. Some of us are drawn to notice the struc-tural elements of a text; others pay closer attention to the sound and cadence of the language. It makes sense to begin with what interests you. As you read through these craft lessons, find the ones that resonate with your aesthetic sense of what makes good writing. Those lessons will fit most naturally with what you know and believe. You might begin there and slowly branch out to other ways of looking at text that extend your way of reading.

Here's a different approach: begin by paying attention to what your stu-dents are already doing. Martha Horn, a teacher and author, says that rather than starting with the list of things she wants to teach, she begins by honor-ing what students are already doing well in their writing. She picks out very specific examples from the students' work that she can lay alongside of pub-lished writing. Sometimes these are very simple connections, but always they are specific to certain elements of craft. Here's what this might look like with one first grader's writing.

The Big Burger in Birmingham

Aaaaaaaaaaaaaaaa . . . It's the big burger in Birmingham.
The mustard. The ketchup. The meat. The bread. The mayonnaise. The
onions. The pickles . . . Then there's only one thing to do, let's . . .
EAT IT!!!
Chomp chomp gulp!
   Rip

Notice the title Rip chose for his story: "The Big Burger in Birmingham." He makes a pattern with the B sound by repeating it three times. Patricia Polacco does this with her book title *Babushka Baba Yaga*. Lynne Cherry makes a different kind of pattern with her title *Armadillo from Amarillo*. Rip chose a title that sounds pleasing to the ear, just as Polacco and Cherry did.

Here's something else. Mem Fox put sound effects right into the story in her book *Night Noises*. Rip does the same thing when he writes, "Aaaaaaaaaaaaaaaa . . ." at the beginning of his story and "Chomp chomp gulp" at the end. Chances are, there are other children in your class who could learn to use alliteration or sound effects.

This book can offer you a way to extend an element of craft that individuals in your class are using (often unknowingly) in their writing. Attend to the writing in front of you; then as you read these craft lessons, begin with those that support and extend the writing your students are already doing. In many cases you'll find that you have examples from your own students to support the lessons we've detailed in this book.

You're likely to begin in the section designated for your grade level, but don't forget to browse the other sections. You'll find lessons there that can be easily modified to fit your students' needs.

Where do these craft lessons fit into my language arts program?

These craft lessons are designed to fit into the mini-lesson component of the writing workshop. But don't limit your thinking to this one time of the day. You'll find that they can also be helpful during a writing conference. These lessons will help you think about individual students' writing in fresh ways. If the moment is right, seize the opportunity to introduce a craft lesson right then and there.

These craft lessons can also enrich the book discussions you have with students. In fact, much of what students learn about the craft of writing takes place *outside* the writing workshop at other times of the day: during literature circles, large-group book discussions, or one-on-one reading conferences. Writing workshop becomes the time for students to act on the information they are learning about craft by trying it out in their own writing.

Is it best to assign these craft lessons or leave them optional?

The point can be argued both ways.

Assign them: yes! These strategies are too important to be left up to the student's whim. If we always make them optional, students won't take them seriously, and some students will never try them out. Certain kids will simply never see the power of using the five senses, or trying various leads, unless we require them to try it at least once.

Assign them: no! If we do that, it becomes *our* workshop instead of theirs. A student will no longer sit down and consider, What am I working on now? Instead he'll look up and consider, What does she want us to do today?

This is a judgment call only you can make. We know excellent teachers who would line up on both sides of the question. We believe that a strong classroom environment includes a great deal of student choice. This includes the decision about what writing strategy to use, and when to use it. There may be occasions when you want all students to try out a particular strategy. But in general, these craft lessons should be presented as options for students to use if and when they see fit. Ideally, your classroom has the kind of environment where you put forth lots of rich writing ideas and your students are willing to try them out.

What about the students who don't take up the invitation?

Not all children will be ready to try each new element of craft the day you present it. But there are ways to keep the idea alive so that when they *are* ready, they'll be reminded to give it a try.

One way is to create a place in the classroom that can remind students to explore the element of craft. For example, you might design a bulletin board that lists various kinds of endings, and ask students to add models of each as they find them in the books they are reading, or as they experiment in their own writing. This sets up an after-image of your lesson and will help extend its usefulness to more students in the workshop.

There are other ways to encourage more students to attempt the lesson you are teaching. Let's face it: teaching a mini-lesson can be like lighting a match—it burns brightly for a little while but quickly burns out. The danger in mini-lessons is *mentioning* instead of *teaching*.

You can reinforce a mini-lesson by returning to the element of craft at the end of the writing time. Designate a corner of the blackboard where the craft element gets highlighted, and have students sign their names after they try it in their writing. At the end of the writing time, remind students what you discussed with them during the mini-lesson. Find out which students tried out the idea in their own writing, and start your share session by asking a few of those students to read aloud their writing.

You might also use a large easel pad to record discussions and demonstrations. This allows you and your students to refer back to earlier lessons about craft and apply them at a later time. It also provides a personalized record of the craft elements you have taught over the course of the year. Next year's class will be unique and will influence what you teach about craft and the way you'll teach it. Still, it will be useful to have an archive of your own lessons to draw from.

You put forth all these elements of craft. Great, but how do I keep myself organized?

You might keep a notebook to record the various mini-lessons you share with students. At the end of each lesson, and during the workshop as you observe students writing, you can keep notes of follow-up ideas that will help you continue to develop your students' understanding of the element of craft at hand.

Good mini-lessons are generative. We rediscovered this fact as we were writing this book. One lesson led to another. In fact, the temptation was often strong to roll too many ideas into a single lesson.

Rarely does an element of craft get taught in a single lesson. If you introduce the concept of leads one day, you'll want to return to this topic a number of times from a variety of perspectives. Though there is no set sequence to the many lessons you might do on leads, a spiral of craft lessons might look like this:

- **Day One**—Introduce the one-sentence lead.

- **Day Two**—Teach students to read a piece looking for where the lead ends.

- **Day Three**—Demonstrate how the lead can be a way to introduce one of the elements (character, conflict, setting) of the story.

These lessons may or may not take place on consecutive days. While some teachers might present successive lessons on a single element, others prefer to intersperse lessons on a single element among other aspects of craft. Either way, you'll want to spiral back to the subject and build on what students have already learned. The notebook will help you organize the process for doing this.

As you read this book you can use your notebook to jot down your own extensions to the lessons you read. As you read our discussions, you'll think of books your students already know that fit the purpose. Or you may conceive of a totally different way to demonstrate the idea. Your notebook can be a place to develop mini-lessons of your own. Use our craft lessons as a springboard into your own.

I talk a lot to my students about qualities of good writing, but they seldom apply it to their own work. Suggestions?

Those of us who work with young writers need to continually think about *how* we articulate each craft lesson. A teacher encourages her students to "Be descriptive" or "Write a lead that grabs your reader," but such advice may be too general to be of any real use. The student is left to wonder: "Great! But how?"

It's important for us to break down general advice into specifics that our students can use. Rather than telling students, "Be descriptive," you could suggest, "Try to use your five senses when you describe a person, place, or thing." Rather than advising, "Write a lead that grabs your reader," you could say, "Try starting right in the middle of the story."

We all know it's easier to recognize good writing when we see it than to produce it ourselves. Developing an awareness may be the first step toward gaining control over craft, but students who want to try something new may stumble over how to do it. When you teach an element of craft, you'll often want to accompany it with a process strategy.

Let's say you present students with a craft lesson on using physical description to develop characters. Students may recognize when writers do it and even imagine what they might include in stories of their own. But for young writers who haven't learned how to insert, delete, or reorder words on paper, it may be impossible to bring this strategy to their own writing. Teaching students how to use a caret, asterisk, arrow, or spider flap (a page or strip of paper taped on the side to provide room for adding detail) will give them a concrete way to apply this craft lesson to their own writing.

How much can I expect my students to learn about craft in a single year?

Don't get too ambitious. If you can really teach your students two or three things about craft in a single year, strategies that become part of their repertoires as writers, you've probably done well.

Build on those writing elements you consider most important. Perhaps you are drawn to discuss character development, or the architecture of a story. In order for students to learn to handle these well, you'll need to return to these elements of craft again and again during the school year.

You have said that these craft lessons can also be used during individual writing conferences. How many craft lessons can you reasonably teach during a single conference?

One.

Most of us had ambitious teachers when we went to school. True, they may have assigned us to write infrequently, but they sure did try to get lots of mileage from each assignment. In every paper we wrote they corrected run-ons, paragraphing, spelling, word choice, organization, grammar, and so on.

This wasn't all bad. Teaching skills in the context of students' personal writing is far better than teaching them in isolation. But as teachers, it's important for us to set limits. *Our ability to teach skills in any given piece of writing nearly always outlasts the student's interest in the writing.* A student whose eyes have glazed over is trying to tell us, "Enough already!"

We believe that it's best to write frequently with students but try to teach just one thing in each piece of writing. Most learners can absorb only a limited number of new ideas at any given time. Squeeze it once and let the student go on to the next piece of writing.

If you could suggest just one thing, the single best thing I could do to improve the quality of writing in my classroom, what would it be?

■ Write with your students.

■ Read with your students.

■ And make plenty of time to talk together about the reading and writing you're doing.

Appendixes

APPENDIX 1

Emily's Story

My Nana is everything to me. She does everything to spoil me. But that is not why I like her. I like Nana because she is nice and calm. She is sweet and gentle. I like to do puzzles with Nana. Nana plays with me all the time. We have fun together. I like to watch movies with Nana. She is so much fun to be around. My favorite food that Nana makes is her soup with pistena! Nana makes me soup when I come over her house. It smells good and makes me more hungry! I love my Nana! My Nana is everything.

Me

> I'm 8-m years old I play
> soccer and baseball. I have a
> sister dog cats Mom and Dad. I live
> in Epping New Hampshire. I get
> comfoused at math. I'm loving
> to my Mom Dad cats Dog and my
> sister. I am talkative to my loving
> Family. I am a hardworking kid at math
> I was excited when I went to
> wrestling. I am kind to my Mom
> sister cats dog and my only Dad.
> I am funny to my sister.

Mark (second grade)

K-2 New Ways to Write About an Old Topic
p. 41

Firefly

(a song)

A little light is going by,
Is going up to see the sky,
A little light with wings.

I never would have thought of it,
To have a little bug all lit,
And made to go on wings.

> *Elizabeth Madox Roberts,*
> Piping Down the Valleys Wild

K-2 Focus: Staying on the Topic p. 44

Changing a Tire

I was in the car with my mother and my big sister. Mom was driving. We were going to McDonalds which I think has the best French fries, even though my sister likes Burger King fries. The car started shaking and Mom had to pull over. We had a flat tire. My sister didn't want to help change it. She just sat and read her tennis magazine. All she thinks about is tennis. She is saving up her money so she can go to tennis camp this summer. I want to go to soccer camp. I'm already on the travel team. Anyway, Mom didn't know how to change the tire so I helped. Dad showed me how. Dad is good at fixing things. He even fixed a window after I broke it. It wasn't really my fault because I hit the ball right to Josh but he fell and missed it and it hit the window.

I told Mom to get out the jack. We jacked up the car. Then the hard part—we had to get the lug nuts loose. My sister wouldn't help. She turned on the radio and found a station that plays country music. I hate country music. The music I like is rock. I want to be a musician when I grow up. Mom helped me get the tire out of the back but she got her pants all covered with black stuff. My hands got dirty, too, but I didn't care. I knew Dad would be proud of me. Actually I think I want to be a deep sea explorer when I grow up because you get to explore wrecks. There's a bunch of gold sitting on the bottom of the sea, and I'm going to find it.

My Dog

He pushed his wet nose
against my cheek.
I remember my dog.

He liked to catch leaves
when they fell off the trees.
I remember my dog.

At night I felt safe
when he slept near me.
I remember my dog.

Seth Reed (second grade)

Using Cut and Paste p. 58

A Change in the Weather

We were on vacation in Hawaii. My Dad had rented a condo right on the beach. Every morning we saw people on boats cruising past our condo. Sometimes they waved. Dad explained to me that you could rent boats like that. My sister and I kept begging my parents to rent a boat so we could go way out on the water. Finally, on the fourth day of the vacation, Dad agreed to rent the boat. We got up early and went out on the ocean. The boat was real nice. It had a cabin, a bathroom, and a cooler filled with ice and soda.

All morning we had a terrific time sunning and cruising around.* But around two o'clock the skies clouded up. A hot wind blew up off the land. In less than fifteen minutes there were whitecaps on the water, and our boat was rocking like crazy back and forth.

"Looks like a storm," Dad said. "We'd better head in."

"I don't feel so good," my little brother said. "Can't you make the boat stop tipping?"

"Hang on," Dad told us. "We'll be back soon."

He headed the boat toward shore, but the waves got bigger. A wave washed over the back of the boat. After that Dad said we'd better stay down below or with him in the cabin. The sky had turned a strange color, half-green and half-black. I had to remind myself that it was still the middle of the day! It was only a few miles to the shore, but it took us almost an hour to get back. I can't begin to tell you how glad I was to get out of that boat!

My Stepfather, Rowdy

My stepfather's name is Rowdy (actually it's his nickname) and he's the best. He's real nice to me. I always have a blast when I go over his house.

Food is one big difference between my dad and Rowdy. At my dad's house there's nothing but healthy snacks in the fridge. I bet the FBI could search his house and still not find one speck of chocolate. Rowdy's got nothing against junk food. In every room there are bowls of delicious treats. Our favorite thing to do at night is watch videos and PIG OUT!

Like I said, Rowdy is a good guy. Whenever I ask my dad if I can do stuff, or borrow something from the garage, he's like, no way. But at Rowdy's house he let's me do all kinds of things, almost anything I want. If I want to use some tool or piece of equipment in his garage, he's like: "Go for it." Rowdy's got lots of cool stuff in his basement, too, mostly things he doesn't need. He let's me go down there and poke around. I've found some great junk in the boxes down there.

Rowdy was in the Marines. He keeps bunches of army collectibles and war antiques in two chests up in his attic. Rowdy lets me go up there and play with that stuff whenever I want. He says he's going to give me some when I'm older.

My dad is Mr. Serious all the time. Rowdy likes to goof around with me and Mom when we're cooking supper or just hanging out. He brings me lots of fun places, too. And sometimes he does funny tricks that really crack me up. Like I said, Rowdy is the best.

Learning to Ride My Bike

I think everybody who can, should learn to ride a bike. A bike with two wheels, that is. I got my chance in first grade. My dad, my sister, and I went to a soccer field behind my school: Chapman. My dad boosted me on to my training wheel-less bicycle. He held the back of my seat and ran with me for a few paces and let go. I was riding! I was riding by myself on a two wheeler! But then I fell down. As I got up on my bike my dad said I should pedal when I ride. In the next half an hour I could stay balanced pedaling. Then my dad told me to try and steer. I went ahead and steered right into the ground.

The next few weeks were smothered in blood, scabs, bruises and Band-Aids. But at the end, triumph. I could ride a two wheeler.

Waking Joseph

I go into Joseph's bed to wake him up. His face is poking out above the covers, eyes shut. He is four years old. I use a soft voice: "Time to get up, Jo Jo."

Joseph opens his eyes, frowns, and buries his head under the covers. I hear his muffled voice:

"I'm not Joseph. I'm not a boy."

"Oh," I say. "Are you an animal?"

"Yeah," he answers. I know this game. Now I have to guess what kind of animal.

"Are you a beaver?" (No.) "Are you a giraffe?" (Nope.) It takes about fifteen guesses before I find out what he is—a baby seal. Now I ask:

"Well, did you have any dreams, Baby Seal?"

He nods and tells me all about his dream. After he's finished telling me, I ask if he's ready to get up.

"You forgot something," he says, and he's right. I make the fingers from one of my hands walk across the bedspread toward Joseph. He starts smiling as they approach. I make the fingers talk to him in a high, funny voice:

"Is it a Tickle Day or a Not-Tickle Day?" they ask.

"A Tickle Day," he answers with a big smile.

"Great!" the fingers say. They turn and walk back across the bedspread to where the fingers from my other hand are waiting.

"What did he say?" the fingers ask.

"He said it was a Tickle Day!" the first fingers say. Joseph grins as all the fingers start dancing with each other. Then they stop, turn, and scamper back toward Joseph. He draws back, waiting, and all of a sudden they leap to tickle him under his chin.

Using Paragraphs to Organize Your Writing p. 71

Sleepover Party (without paragraphs)

It was my birthday and mom said I could have a sleep over party with four friends. Mom asked me a bunch of questions like what did I want for dinner, what movie should we rent, and what kind of cake? The day before the party we went shopping for snacks. We bought Reese's Peanut Butter Cups, Twizzlers, and cheese puffs. Finally the day came. Trevor, Ryan, Alex, and Luis came home after school. We played baseball in the backyard for hours, had pizza, and then settled down to watch our movie. After a while we started looking for the Reese's Peanut Butter Cups. We looked everywhere but couldn't find them until Luis noticed they were in the bag on top of the heater. We all reached in to grab some. They were smooshy and melted, but still good. Our hands were covered so we cleaned up in the bathroom. By the time we were done, we had chocolate on everything. When the movie was over we turned off the light and tried to sleep. Right away Ryan started telling jokes like he always does and we started laughing like crazy. We couldn't stop. Finally we did. It was 3:00 a.m. before we stopped laughing. Then Mom yelled downstairs, "Wake up! Pancakes." It felt like one minute had gone by but it was nine o'clock in the morning. We went upstairs and sat around the table fighting over who would get the next pancake. Mom kept cooking pancakes until we were stuffed. Ryan started telling jokes again, but this time we were too full or too tired to laugh. We just said, "Save it for later." Pretty soon everyone's parents came. When they were all gone, Mom asked if I wanted more pancakes. I told her no and went back to bed.

Using Paragraphs to Organize Your Writing p. 71

Sleepover Party (revised)

It was my birthday and mom said I could have a sleep over party with four friends. Mom asked me a bunch of questions like what did I want for dinner, what movie should we rent, and what kind of cake? The day before the party we went shopping for snacks. We bought Reese's Peanut Butter Cups, Twizzlers, and cheese puffs.

Finally the day came. Trevor, Ryan, Alex, and Luis came home after school. We played baseball in the backyard for hours, had pizza, and then settled down to watch our movie. After a while we started looking for the Reese's Peanut Butter Cups. We looked everywhere but couldn't find them until Luis noticed they were in the bag on top of the heater. We all reached in to grab some. They were smooshy and melted, but still good. Our hands were covered so we cleaned up in the bathroom. By the time we were done, we had chocolate on everything.

When the movie was over we turned off the light and tried to sleep. Right away Ryan started telling jokes like he always does and we started laughing like crazy. We couldn't stop. Finally we did. It was 3:00 a.m. before we stopped laughing. Then Mom yelled downstairs, "Wake up! Pancakes." It felt like one minute had gone by but it was nine o'clock in the morning.

We went upstairs and sat around the table fighting over who would get the next pancake. Mom kept cooking pancakes until we were stuffed. Ryan started telling jokes again, but this time we were too full or too tired to laugh. We just said, "Save it for later." Pretty soon everyone's parents came. When they were all gone, Mom asked if I wanted more pancakes. I told her no and went back to bed.

Craft Lessons: Teaching Writing K–8 SECOND EDITION

The Inner Life of a Character p. 74

Spot

Once there was a kid. His name was Dave. Dave was a small boy for his age. He had no friends. But he wanted one desperately! It was really close to Christmas. He was sad and didn't know what he wanted from Santa. Just then a thought came to his mind. He could ask Santa for a dog and that could be his friend. So he hurried downstairs to get a pen and paper. Then he ran upstairs to write a letter to Santa. Then he got an envelope and put the paper in it and sealed it shut. He put a stamp on the envelope and mailed it to the North Pole.

In two more days it would be Christmas. The two days had passed and it was Christmas morning! Dave ran downstairs and there was a little puppy in a basket with a red ribbon around his neck. He was all white with a big black spot on his forehead, so Dave named him Spot. From then on he was never lonely. The puppy grew up to be a huge dog. And Dave was happy from then on because he had a friend.

Wade Christopher (third grade)

Staying on Topic p. 80

The Salt Marsh

On May 1 our class went on a field trip to a salt marsh. I used to know a kid named Mike Marsh except some kids called him Marshmallow Boy because he was kind've fat, which I know was mean. We met at the school at 7 am. First thing we did was stop for breakfast. I had a "Breakfast Bullet"—a sandwich with egg and cheese and ham and bacon—which was wicked tasty!

When we got there we met our marsh guide, a man named Mr. Eggers. He made us slather on bug spray because the marsh is full of mosquitoes. We started walking through a path, surrounded by tall grass. Mr. Eggers said we might see some wildlife and we did. We saw red-winged blackbirds, crabs, two pretty big snakes, and some moles. We also found some trash like regular Coke cans and some empty cans of diet Coke. Honestly, I can't see how people can drink diet soda—it tastes all chemically to me.

Anyway, Mr. Eggers taught us about the marsh, and you could tell he really loved that place. When I first got there the marsh seemed pretty pointless. You can't build a house on it. You can't play in it like you can at Prescott Park. (Prescott Park is close to my house but it's closed right now due to repairs.) But Mr. Eggers described the salt marsh as a place where the ocean and the land shake hands with each other. He taught us that salt marshes work like giant sponges, soaking up sea water, or excess rain. They prevent flooding. Not only that, they provide food and habitat for thousands of birds and fish and other animals. The salt marsh seemed like nothing more than a bunch of mud and boring grass, but after listening to that man I realized it's actually one of the most important places on our planet.

3-4   The Circular Ending p. 82

My Grandpa

My Grandpa is not around.
I loved him.
He used to give me candy.
He takes me places.
He used to take me swimming.
He delivered me and my sister and brother.
I liked when he held me.
My Grandpa is not around.

Jeanine Cozzens (third grade)

My Pet Dog

Four years ago I got a dog. Her name was Shyana. I loved her very much, but there was one problem. We had to chain her up on my basketball goal and we knew that was wrong. So we let her in the basement until we got home. That was not good. She tore up everything. So then we let her stay upstairs, but she tore a hole in the carpet and we had to give her up. I was sad but it was for her own good. I really miss her and I am planning to ask the lady for my dog back. I can't stop remembering when she was my alarm clock. She licked my face and woke me up on the first day we got her. I tried not to remember that when I woke up and she was gone.

Derek (second grade)

Combining Short Sentences p. 87

Looking at Compound Sentences

You might invite students to look closely at the following sentences and, if they like them, copy them into their writer's notebooks.

"The puppy had been abandoned, and it made its way down the road toward the Lacey's small house, its ears tucked, its tail between its legs, shivering." (Cynthia Rylant, *Every Living Thing*, p. 42)

"Because the roads would be too bad for travel for many days, Mr. Lacey couldn't get out to take the puppy to the pound in the city right away." (same, p. 43)

"Words are used to think with, to write with, to dream with, to hope and pray with." (Andrew Clements, *Frindle*, p. 100)

"When I was done, Otis thanked me." (Kate DiCamillo, *Because of Winn-Dixie*, p. 84)

"He was an ugly dog, but already, I loved him with all my heart." (same, p. 14)

"Harry was several streets away before he collapsed onto a low wall in Magnolia Crescent, panting from the effort of dragging his trunk. He sat quite still, anger still surging through him, listening to the frantic thumping of his heart." (J. K. Rowling, *Harry Potter and the Prisoner of Azkaban*, p. 31)

Pruning the Bushes—Cutting What You Don't Need p. 96

Clamming

A few nights ago I was cleaning my garage. It had been months since I'd tackled that unpleasant job, and I had a big pile of junk to sort through. While going through broken lawn chairs and dilapidated croquet sets, I came across a metal clam basket. This reminded me of the summers I spent digging clams when I was in college.

On clamming days my brother and I got up at dawn. The black of night was just beginning to lighten when we staggered out of bed. Clamming was hard physical labor, and it was murder on your hands. Sometimes the muscles in one of my hands were knotted up, the fingers clamped into a fist. I stood in the bathroom rubbing the muscles until they loosened enough for me to hold my toothbrush.

Jimmy and I didn't talk much in the morning. In the kitchen, we each filled a thermos with lemonade, and made a huge lunch: thick roast beef sandwiches, chips, pretzels, bananas, apples, a wedge of pound cake. I never ate much in the morning, and all that food made me queasy but it was important to make a big lunch. Clamming was hard work, and by eleven I'd be ravenous.

The sun still hadn't come up yet as we loaded our boat and started the engine. Jimmy steered the boat down the canal while I worked the bilge pump.

On those mornings we never thought about how important clamming was to the South Shore of Long Island. We clammed on the Great South Bay, and the clams we harvested were served by fine restaurants all over the country. Clamming was an important business for that area. It was just a summer job for us, but it also provided work for hundreds of professional "bay men" as they were called.

When we reached the bay, Jimmy pushed the throttle and headed us straight toward a cluster of clam boats.

"They must have found a school of clams," Jimmy said as we pulled up near the boats. This was an old clam joke since clams don't move in schools, hardly move at all.

"Hey!" Joey Greco called. "Watch the wake!"

I smiled at him. Joey was a kid we saw every day on the bay. I also knew him from school. He had moved from Illinois a few years ago. His father worked as an electrician.

"Sorry, sorry," I said, throwing in our anchor.

"You guys better go home," Joey groused. "I just dug the last clam in the bay. There's no more left."

5-8   Pruning the Bushes—Cutting What You Don't Need p. 96

Clamming

~~A few nights ago I was cleaning my garage. It had been months since I'd tackled that unpleasant job, and I had a big pile of junk to sort through. While going through broken lawn chairs and dilapidated croquet sets, I came across a metal clam basket. This reminded me of the summers I spent digging clams when I was in college.~~

On clamming days my brother and I got up at dawn. The black of night was just beginning to lighten when we staggered out of bed. Clamming was hard physical labor, and it was murder on your hands. Sometimes the muscles in one of my hands were knotted up, the fingers clamped into a fist. I stood in the bathroom rubbing the muscles until they loosened enough for me to hold my toothbrush.

Jimmy and I didn't talk much in the morning. In the kitchen, we each filled a thermos with lemonade, and made a huge lunch: thick roast beef sandwiches, chips, pretzels, bananas, apples, a wedge of pound cake. I never ate much in the morning, and all that food made me queasy but it was important to make a big lunch. Clamming was hard work, and by eleven I'd be ravenous.

The sun still hadn't come up yet as we loaded our boat and started the engine. Jimmy steered the boat down the canal while I worked the bilge pump.

~~On those mornings we never thought about how important clamming was to the South Shore of Long Island. We clammed on the Great South Bay, and the clams we harvested were served by fine restaurants all over the country. Clamming was an important business for that area. It was just a summer job for us, but it also provided work for hundreds of professional "bay men" as they were called.~~

When we reached the bay, Jimmy pushed the throttle and headed us straight toward a cluster of clam boats.

"They must have found a school of clams," Jimmy said as we pulled up near the boats. This was an old clam joke since clams don't move in schools, hardly move at all.

"Hey!" Joey Greco called. "Watch the wake!"

I smiled at him. Joey was a kid we saw every day on the bay. I also knew him from school. ~~He had moved from Illinois a few years ago. His father worked as an electrician.~~

"Sorry, sorry," I said, throwing in our anchor.

"You guys better go home," Joey groused. "I just dug the last clam in the bay. There's no more left."

5-8 Pruning the Bushes—Cutting What You Don't Need p. 96

Clamming (revised)

On clamming days my brother and I got up at dawn. The black of night was just beginning to lighten when we staggered out of bed. Clamming was hard physical labor, and it was murder on your hands. Sometimes the muscles in one of my hands were knotted up, the fingers clamped into a tight fist. I stood in the bathroom rubbing the muscles until they loosened enough for me to hold my toothbrush.

Jimmy and I didn't talk much in the morning. In the kitchen, we each filled a thermos with lemonade, and made a huge lunch: thick roast beef sandwiches, chips, pretzels, bananas, apples, a wedge of pound cake. I never ate much in the morning, and all that food made me queasy, but it was important to make a big lunch. I knew by eleven I'd be ravenous.

The sun still hadn't come up yet as we loaded our boat and started the engine. Jimmy steered the boat down the canal while I worked the bilge pump.

When we reached the bay, Jimmy pushed the throttle and headed us straight toward a cluster of clam boats.

"They must have found a school of clams," Jimmy said as we pulled up near the boats. This was an old clam joke since clams don't move in schools, hardly move at all.

"Hey!" Joey Greco called. "Watch the wake!"

I smiled at him. Joey was a kid we saw every day on the bay. I also knew him from school.

"Sorry, sorry," I said, throwing in our anchor.

"You guys better go home," Joey groused. "I just dug the last clam in the bay. There's no more left."

Craft Lessons: Teaching Writing K–8 SECOND EDITION

Categories of Leads

Posing a Question

Have you ever imagined what it would be like to play in the NBA? To glide down the court, matching strides with the greatest basketball players in the world? To hear the roar of the crowd as you throw down a dunk, or swat an opponent's shot into the bleachers?

It's every kid's dream.

And for the fortunate few who make it to the NBA, it's a dream come true.

> *Joseph Layden and James Preller,* NBA Game Day

Arresting Sentence

They murdered him.

> *Robert Cormier,* The Chocolate War

Astonishing Fact

Try to imagine a star so big that it would fill all of the solar system within the orbit of Earth, which is 93 million miles from the Sun. A star so turbulent that its eruptions would spread a cloud of gases spanning four light-years, the distance from the Sun to the nearest star. A star so powerful that it glows with the energy of 10 million suns, making it the brightest ever observed in our galaxy, the Milky Way.

> *John Noble Wilford, "At the Core of the Milky Way, the Brightest Star Ever Seen"*

Spoken Words

"Your father has met with an accident."

> *Avi,* The Barn

Setting the Mood

A thin crescent moon, high in the sky, shed faint white light over Dimwood Forest. Stars glowed. Breezes full of ripe summer fragrance floated over nearby meadow and hill. Dimwood itself, veiled in darkness, lay utterly still.

> *Avi,* Poppy

Quotes About Leads

Every lead is a compressed draft. It reveals the subject, the writer's attitude toward the subject, the voice, the direction, the form and order of a piece of writing.

Donald Murray, Shoptalk

You can't wait for a paragraph in or a page in or even a line in to gain the readers' attention. You've got to grab them by the lapels in the first paragraph, and by the end of the first page if you don't throw them across the room, you'll lose them.

Blanche McCrary Boyd in Shoptalk

The Farming Life

You're getting tired of the traffic, the strip malls, the helter skelter pace of life in the 'burbs. You've read a few articles about city people who found peace by moving out to the country, out to the fresh air and clean sunshine. You're thinking about buying a farm, a small one, of course, where you could raise a few crops, some animals, a place where you could get back to a simpler life of the land.

Sure.

Think your life would be slower and simpler working on a farm? Think again! Farming is one of the hardest professions around. Farmers often put in fifteen to eighteen hour workdays, and the days are filled with frustrations and challenges. Busted equipment. Animal sickness. Pesticides.

5-8 Writing Low on the "Food Chain"
p. 101

"The Food Chain of Ideas" in Writing

General   Love, War, Hate, Freedom

↑

↓

Specific   Smell of Shaving Cream,
                                           Beard Stubble

5–8   Describing a Character (1) p. 103

Raymond

Hair the color of pencil shavings,
eyes as dark as a night river,
best friend
since fifth grade
when he seemed to stop
growing.

Large enough
to blacken Danny Webb's eye
when he said,
"Hiya, pip-squeak,"
the first day of eighth grade,

small enough
to get into the movies as a kid.

At the Top Hat Café,
gave me one play
on his juke box quarters.

For three nights,
trusted me
with the false teeth
(uppers only)
he found
on a park bench.

In the Tattoo Emporium,
let me help him
pick out the
eagle-holding-thunderbolt
he'd claim for his chest
the day he turned eighteen.

Paul Janeczko, Brickyard Summer

Describing a Character (2) p. 104

From *Yolonda's Genius*

Aunt Tiny had a laugh as rich and flaky as biscuits and gravy. She wore gorgeous clothes—reds so bright and whites so pure and spanking clean. She would fix ribs, baking them slow in the oven and serve them with red beans and steaming rice. She cooked the beans slow, too, with giant slabs of clove-studded onion.

Tiny's hands were pretty as Momma's, only her nails were very long, squared-off at the tips, and polished a shiny red. She ate with delicate bites, nibbling daintily, mincing her way through rib after rib, wiping her mouth with her napkins, not getting any of the barbecue sauce on her blindingly white slacks. She smelled wonderfully of perfume and food. When she surrounded Yolonda in a big, soft hug, Yolonda could have stayed there forever, inhaling Aunt Tiny's sweetness.

Carol Fenner, Yolonda's Genius

From *Harry Potter and the Sorcerer's Stone*

He was almost twice as tall as a normal man and at least five times as wide. He looked simply too big to be allowed, and so wild—long tangles of bushy black hair and beard hid most of his face, he had hands the size of trash can lids, and his feet in their leather boots were like baby dolphins.

J. K. Rowling, Harry Potter and the Sorcerer's Stone

Craft Lessons: Teaching Writing K–8 **SECOND EDITION**

5-8 Using Interior Monologue p. 107

At Bat

The Palominos were down to their last three strikes. Jesse walked up to the plate and stood outside the batter's box, using the bat to bang dirt out of his cleats.

"No batter, no batter," the catcher snorted. Ted ignored him and looked up at the scoreboard. 3–3, bases loaded, bottom of the seventh. He looked out at the mound where Cliff Proctor glared back at him. They were both in ninth grade, but already there was a dark mustache above Cliff's sneering upper lip. The kid looked closer to twenty than fifteen years old. He let fly a big gob of spittle and pounded his glove.

Don't forget to breathe, Ted said to himself as he stepped into the batter's box. Relax. Get comfortable. This kid throws hard but wild. Don't do him any favors by swinging at a bad pitch. Make him throw strikes. The bases are jammed—a walk is as good as a home run. You're not going to get any offspeed junk from this kid. No way. He's way too cocky for that. This kid's gonna bring his fastball and nothing but. C'mon, Cliff Proctor, I'm ready. Show me your heat.

Moving Madness

Let me say flat-out that I really loved my old house in New Jersey. I had a perfect bedroom, the perfect yard, the perfect distance (close enough to walk or bike) to my perfect friends. Okay, so maybe they weren't exactly perfect, but I thought they were pretty cool.

"I love this house," I told my mom. "We're going to live here forever."

But forever didn't last. Her company wanted to transfer her to North Carolina. She'd be getting a better job, fewer hours, for more money. Not only that, but we'd be living close to her sister and my cousins. Even I could see it was a no-brainer. She accepted the new job. But I wasn't happy about having to move.

Mom started packing and making plans, but I went through that summer like it wasn't real. My friends and I went fishing, or hung out at the Rec Center, as usual. We did plenty of sleepovers. We had a wild bonfire on the beach, with flames at least twenty feet high. It was no big deal if I left my baseball glove, beach towel, or fishing pole at another friend's house or in their car. I knew I could always get it tomorrow.

On August 31 I ran out of tomorrows. The big moving truck came at 7:59 in the morning. Before I had eaten breakfast, the movers scooped up all our stuff, leaving the house completely empty. I feel pretty empty, too.

Copyright © 2007

Ralph Fletcher and

JoAnn Portalupi.

Stenhouse Publishers

5-8   Using a Transition Sentence p. 115

Other Examples of Transition Sentences

"A month had gone by since the Village Fair, a month in which a lot of interesting things had happened to Babe."

"As for ma, she was back with the flock, her foot healed, her cough better."

from Babe: The Gallant Pig *by Dick King-Smith*

"Time passed, and the ring fit the little girl's finger, and it seemed, suddenly, that grandfather was an old man."

from The Two of Them *by Aliki*

Another Night

Lights flash
eerily
on the window blinds
past midnight.

Pickup
truck roars
up the long driveway
to our house.

Quickly
my mother
and I rush to bed
pretending to be asleep.

Father
collapses on the couch,
dozes in a drunken stupor, and
makes the usual sleep noises.

Sun rises at dawn.
Good morning, Nebraska.
We're a perfect
farm family.

Gary Manning

Excerpt from "Barry Bonds's Enhancements" by George F. Will

Would that Barry Bonds had retired after the 1998 season. He might be happier than he seems to be in his long trudge toward tainted glory. Certainly everyone who cares about baseball, and about the integrity of athletic competition generally, would be spared the disturbing spectacle of his unlovely approach to Henry Aaron's career record of 755 home runs.

The numbers Bonds had put up before the 1999 season were luminous enough to have guaranteed him first-ballot election to the Hall of Fame. He had 411 home runs, 445 stolen bases—he is now the only "500-500" player in history—eight All-Star selections and eight Gold Glove Awards. He had won three MVP awards and should have won a fourth that was given to a lesser, but less obnoxious, player.

Excerpt from "Barry Bonds's Enhancements" by George F. Will

(same piece with adjectives underlined):

Would that Barry Bonds had retired after the 1998 season. He might be <u>happier</u> than he seems to be in his <u>long</u> trudge toward <u>tainted</u> glory. Certainly everyone who cares about baseball, and about the integrity of <u>athletic</u> competition generally, would be spared the <u>disturbing</u> spectacle of his <u>unlovely</u> approach to Henry Aaron's <u>career</u> record of 755 home runs.

The numbers Bonds had put up before the 1999 season were <u>luminous</u> enough to have guaranteed him <u>first-ballot</u> election to the Hall of Fame. He had 411 home runs, 445 stolen bases—he is now the only "500-500" player in history—eight <u>All-Star</u> selections and eight Gold Glove Awards. He had won three MVP awards and should have won a fourth that was given to a <u>lesser</u>, but <u>less</u> <u>obnoxious</u>, player.

Benefits of the Computer (version 1)

The computer has produced many important changes in our world. Some of these changes are things we take for granted and may not be aware of. This essay will look at how the computer has given people more information, more time, and more ways to keep in touch with other people.

The computer has given people more information. In the old days, people would have to go to the library or look through an encyclopedia to research a subject. Today a person can use a computer to find information from newspapers and books from all over the world.

The computer has given people more time. People who work on a computer don't have to spend hours adding up numbers. Computerized programs do that work for you. This gives people more time to do what they really want.

The computer has given people more ways to keep in touch with other people. Before the computer was invented people would either have to talk, write a letter, or make a phone call to get in touch with other people. Today people can use the computer to email.

In conclusion, the computer has given people more information, more time, and more ways to keep in touch with other people. Without computers, we would not have these benefits. The world is a lot better now that we have computers in our lives.

Benefits of the Computer (version 2)

Unless you've been living on Neptune, you know that the computer has rocked our world. Inventions like the light bulb and the telephone certainly made a difference in society. But ever since computers were invented, well, things have never been the same.

Like lions on an African grassland, computers are exceptionally good at hunting down information. Not long ago the word "researching" would mean months of drudge work for whatever unfortunate soul needed to dig up information. Today, with the marriage of the computer and internet, all that has changed. Sit down at a computer and—voila!—you've got instant access to newspapers around the world, libraries, and powerful information banks (thank you, Google).

The computer is equally good at helping people communicate with each other. Does *anyone* send letters anymore? The computer gives us all kinds of faster, cooler options for getting in touch with people. Email someone in Tonga. IM your cousin in Japan. Video programs like I-Chat allow a young marine in Baghdad to watch his one year old baby in St. Louis blow out the candle on her birthday cake.

PCs, IMs, RAM—it may sound like alphabet soup. But who could argue that the computer has changed forever—and for better—the way we live on planet Earth?

Children's Books

Abercrombie, Barbara. 1990. *Charlie Anderson.* New York: McElderry.

Ackerman, Karen. 1988. *Song and Dance Man.* New York: Knopf.

Agee, Jon. 2005. *Terrific.* New York: Michael di Capua/Hyperion Books for Children.

Aliki. 1979. *The Two of Them.* New York: Greenwillow.

———. 1983. *A Medieval Feast.* New York: Crowell.

———. 1989. *My Five Senses.* New York: Crowell.

Asch, Frank. 1981. *Just Like Daddy.* New York: Prentice-Hall.

Aston, Dianna Hutts. 2006. *An Egg Is Quiet.* San Francisco: Chronicle.

———. 2007. *A Seed Is Sleepy.* San Francisco: Chronicle.

Avi. 1994. *The Barn.* New York: Orchard.

———. 1995. *Poppy.* New York: Orchard.

Babbitt, Natalie. 1975. *Tuck Everlasting.* New York: Farrar, Straus and Giroux.

Bang, Molly. 1985. *Ten, Nine, Eight.* New York: Puffin.

———. 1996. *Goose.* New York: Blue Sky Press/Scholastic.

Barbour, Karen. 1987. *Little Nino's Pizzeria.* San Diego: Harcourt Brace.

Bauer, Caroline Feller. 1981. *My Mom Travels a Lot.* New York: F. Warne.

Bauer, Marion Dane. 1992. *Ghost Eye.* New York: Scholastic.

Baylor, Byrd. 1977. *Guess Who My Favorite Person Is?* New York: Scribner.

Blos, Joan W. 1987. *Old Henry.* New York: Morrow.

Bogart, JoEllen. 1996. *Gifts.* New York: Scholastic.

Brinckloe, Julie. 1985. *Fireflies!* New York: Macmillan.

Brown, Margaret Wise. 1949. *The Important Book.* New York: Harper.

Browne, Anthony. 1984. *Willy the Wimp.* New York: Knopf.

Bunting, Eve. 1994. *Smoky Night.* San Diego: Harcourt Brace.

———. 1997. *On Call Back Mountain.* New York: Blue Sky Press/Scholastic.

Cameron, Ann. 1981. *The Stories Julian Tells.* New York: Pantheon.

———. 1993. *The Most Beautiful Place in the World.* New York: Bullseye.

Capote, Truman. (1956) 1996. *A Christmas Memory.* New York: Knopf.

Carrick, Carol. 2000. *Mothers Are Like That.* New York: Clarion.

Chall, Marsha Wilson. 1992. *Up North at the Cabin.* New York: Lothrop, Lee & Shepard.

Cherry, Lynne. 1994. *Armadillo from Amarillo.* San Diego: Harcourt Brace.

Clements, Andrew. 1996. *Frindle.* New York: Simon & Schuster Books for Young Readers.

Coffelt, Nancy. 2007. *Fred Stays with Me!* New York: Little, Brown.

Cole, Joanna. 1986. The Magic School Bus series. New York: Scholastic.

Coman, Carolyn. 1995. *What Jamie Saw.* Arden, NC: Front Street.

Cormier, Robert. 1974. *The Chocolate War.* New York: Pantheon.

Crews, Donald. 1991. *Bigmama's.* New York: Greenwillow.

———. 1992. *Shortcut.* New York: Greenwillow.

Curtis, Christopher Paul. 1995. *The Watsons Go to Birmingham—1963.* New York: Delacorte.

Dahl, Roald. 1975. *Danny, the Champion of the World.* New York: Knopf.

de Paola, Tomie. 1978. *The Popcorn Book.* New York: Holiday House.

———. 1981. *Now One Foot, Now the Other.* New York: Putnam.

DiCamillo, Kate. 2000. *Because of Winn-Dixie.* Cambridge, MA: Candlewick.

———. 2001. *The Tiger Rising.* Cambridge, MA: Candlewick.

Farmer, Nancy. 2002. *The House of the Scorpion.* New York: Atheneum Books for Young Readers.

Fenner, Carol. 1995. *Yolonda's Genius.* New York: McElderry.

Fleischman, Paul. 1991. *The Borning Room.* New York: HarperCollins.

Fletcher, Ralph. 1995. *Fig Pudding.* New York: Clarion.

———. 1997. *Twilight Comes Twice.* New York: Clarion.

———. 1998. *Flying Solo.* New York: Clarion.

———. 2003. *Hello, Harvest Moon.* New York: Clarion.

———. 2005. *Marshfield Dreams.* New York: Henry Holt.

———. 2007. *The One O'Clock Chop.* New York: Henry Holt.

Fox, Mem. 1989a. *Koala Lou.* San Diego: Harcourt Brace.

———. 1989b. *Night Noises.* San Diego: Harcourt Brace.

———. 1990. *Guess What?* San Diego: Harcourt Brace.

Fritz, Jean. 1982. *Homesick, My Own Story.* New York: Putnam.

Gardiner, John Reynolds. 2003. *Stone Fox.* New York: HarperTrophy.

Garland, Sherry. 1993. *The Lotus Seed.* San Diego: Harcourt Brace.

Gipson, Fred. 2001. *Old Yeller.* New York: Perennial Classics.

Gray, Libba Moore. 1999. *My Mama Had a Dancing Heart.* New York: Orchard.

Greenfield, Eloise. 1978. *Honey, I Love.* New York: Crowell.

———. 1988. *Grandpa's Face.* New York: Philomel.

Hanson, Mary. 2002. *The Difference Between Babies and Cookies.* San Diego: Silver Whistle/Harcourt.

Harrington, Janice N. 2004. *Going North.* New York: Melanie Kroupa.

Hawes, Judy. 1991. *Fireflies in the Night.* New York: Crowell.

Heard, Georgia. 1992. "Song of the Dolphin" and "Eagle Flight." In *Creatures of Earth, Sea, and Sky: Poems.* Honesdale, PA: Wordsong.

Henkes, Kevin. 1989. *Chester's Way.* New York: Puffin.

———. 1990. *Julius, the Baby of the World.* New York: Greenwillow.

———. 1991. *Chrysanthemum.* New York. Greenwillow.

———. 1996. *Lilly's Purple Plastic Purse.* New York: Greenwillow.

———. 2003. *Olive's Ocean.* New York: Greenwillow.

———. 2004. *Kitten's First Full Moon.* New York: Greenwillow.

———. 2007. *A Good Day.* New York: Greenwillow.

Hesse, Karen. 1994. *Phoenix Rising.* New York: Holt.

———. 1997. *Out of the Dust.* New York: Scholastic.

Hessell, Jenny. 1990. *Staying at Sam's.* New York: Lippincott.

Houston, Gloria. 1992. *My Great-Aunt Arizona.* New York: HarperCollins.

Hughes, Langston. 1986. "Poem." In *Best Friends*, ed. Lee Bennett Hopkins. New York: Harper and Row.

———. 1996. "Passing." In *A Way Out of No Way*, ed. Jacqueline Woodson. New York: Holt.

Hughes, Ted. (1968) 1995. *The Iron Giant.* (British title: *The Iron Man.*) New York: Harper and Row.

Hutchins, Pat. 1986. *The Doorbell Rang.* New York: Greenwillow.

———. 1993. *Titch.* New York: Aladdin.

Isadora, Rachel. 1998. *A South African Night.* New York: Geenwillow.

Janeczko, Paul. 1989. "Raymond." In *Brickyard Summer.* New York: Orchard.

Johnson, Angela. 1992. *The Leaving Morning.* New York: Orchard.

Johnson, D. B. 2000. *Henry Hikes to Fitchburg.* Boston: Houghton Mifflin.

Juster, Norton. 2005. *The Hello, Goodbye Window.* New York: Michael di Capua/Hyperion Books for Children.

King-Smith, Dick. 2005. *Babe: The Gallant Pig.* New York: Random House.

Kraus, Robert. 1970. *Whose Mouse Are You?* New York: Macmillan.

———. 1986. *Where Are You Going, Little Mouse?* New York: Morrow.

Krull, Kathleen. 1996. *Wilma Unlimited.* San Diego: Harcourt Brace.

Kumin, Maxine. 1964. *Beach Before Breakfast.* New York: Putnam.

Lasky, Kathryn. 1997. *Pond Year.* Cambridge, MA: Candlewick Press.

Layden, Joseph, and James Preller. 1997. *NBA Game Day.* New York: Scholastic.

Lessac, Frane. 1984. *My Little Island.* New York: Lippincott.

Lester, Julius. 1994. *John Henry.* New York: Dial.

London, Jonathan. 1998. *Dream Weaver.* San Diego: Silver Whistle.

Long, Melinda. 2003. *How I Became a Pirate.* San Diego: Harcourt Brace.

Lyon, George Ella. 1991. *Cecil's Story.* New York: Orchard.

MacLachlan, Patricia. 1980. *Arthur for the Very First Time.* New York: Harper and Row.

———. 1985. *Sarah, Plain and Tall.* New York: Harper and Row.

———. 1995. *What You Know First.* New York: HarperCollins.

Marshak, Suzanna. 1991. *I Am the Ocean.* New York: Little, Brown.

Martin, Bill, Jr., and John Archambault. 1986. *White Dynamite and Curly Kidd.* New York: Holt, Rinehart, and Winston.

Martinez, Victor. 1996. *Parrot in the Oven: Mi Vida.* New York: HarperCollins.

McMullan, Kate, and Jim McMullan. 2002. *I Stink!* New York: Joanne Cotler.

———. 2006. *I'm Dirty!* New York: Joanne Cotler.

McNaughton, Colin. 1995. *Suddenly!* San Diego: Harcourt Brace.

McPhail, David. 2004. *My Little Brother.* Orlando, FL: Harcourt.

Mitchell, Margaree King. 1993. *Uncle Jed's Barbershop.* New York: Simon and Schuster Books for Young Readers.

Munsch, Robert. 1999. *We Share Everything.* New York: Scholastic.

Naylor, P. R. 1991. *Shiloh.* New York: Atheneum.

Nolan, Han. 1997. *Dancing on the Edge.* New York: Harcourt Brace.

Numeroff, Laura. 1992. *If You Give a Mouse a Cookie.* New York: HarperFestival.

Nye, Naomi Shihab. 1994. *Sitti's Secrets.* New York: Four Winds.

Park, Barbara. 2006. *Mick Harte Was Here.* New York: Yearling.

Park, Linda Sue. 2005. *Bee-bim Bop!* New York: Clarion.

Parr, Todd. 2004. *The Peace Book.* New York: Little, Brown.

Paulsen, Gary. 1990. *Woodsong.* New York: Simon and Schuster.

———. 1999. *Hatchet.* New York: Aladdin.

Philbrick, Rodman. 1993. *Freak the Mighty.* New York: Scholastic.

Pilkey, Dav. 1996. *The Paperboy.* New York: Orchard.

Polacco, Patricia. 1990. *Thunder Cake.* New York: Philomel.

———. 1992a. *Chicken Sunday.* New York: Philomel.

———. 1992b. *Mrs. Katz and Tush.* New York: Bantam.

———. 1993. *Babushka Baba Yaga.* New York: Philomel.

———. 1994. *My Rotten Redheaded Older Brother.* New York: Simon and Schuster.

Raschka, Chris. 1998. *Arlene Sardine.* New York: Orchard.

Rathmann, Peggy. 1994. *Good Night, Gorilla.* New York: Putnam.

———. 1995. *Officer Buckle and Gloria.* New York: Putnam.

Reiser, Lynn. 1992. *Any Kind of Dog.* New York: Greenwillow.

———. 1996. *Beach Feet.* New York: Greenwillow.

Ringgold, Faith. 1991. *Tar Beach.* New York: Crown.

Roberts, Elizabeth Madox. 1982. "Firefly." In *Piping Down the Valleys Wild*, ed. Nancy Larrick. New York: Dell Yearling.

Rowling, J. K.1998. *Harry Potter and the Sorcerer's Stone.* New York: Arthur A. Levine.

———. 1999. *Harry Potter and the Prisoner of Azkaban.* New York: Arthur A. Levine.

Rylant, Cynthia. 1982. *When I Was Young in the Mountains.* New York: Dutton.

———. 1985. "Slower Than the Rest." In *Every Living Thing.* New York: Bradbury.

———. 1986. *Night in the Country.* New York: Bradbury.

———. 1987. *Birthday Presents.* New York: Orchard.

———. 1988. *Every Living Thing.* New York: Aladdin.

———. 1994. *Henry and Mudge and the Happy Cat.* New York: Aladdin.

———. 1997. *Cat Heaven.* New York: Blue Sky Press.

———. 1998. *Scarecrow.* San Diego. Harcourt

———. 2000. *In November.* San Diego. Harcourt.

———. 2002. *The Ticky-Tacky Doll.* San Diego: Harcourt.

Sachar, Louis. 1998. *Holes.* New York: Farrar, Straus and Giroux.

Say, Allen. 1993. *Grandfather's Journey.* Boston: Houghton Mifflin.

Seuss, Dr. 1961. *The Sneetches and Other Stories.* New York: Random House.

Shannon, David. 1998. *No, David!* New York: Blue Sky Press.

———. 2006. *Good Boy, Fergus!* New York: Blue Sky Press.

Siebert, Diane. 1991. *Sierra.* New York: HarperCollins.

Simont, Marc. 1997. *The Goose That Almost Got Cooked.* New York: Scholastic.

Soto, Gary. 1990. "Broken Chain." In *Baseball in April and Other Stories*. San Diego: Harcourt Brace.

Spinelli, Jerry. 1997. *Wringer*. New York: HarperCollins.

Steig, William. 1971. *Amos and Boris*. New York: Farrar, Straus and Giroux.

———. 1986. *Brave Irene*. New York: Farrar, Straus and Giroux.

———. 1990. *Shrek!* New York: Farrar, Straus and Giroux.

Steptoe, John. (1969) 1987. *Stevie*. New York: Harper and Row.

Stevens, Janet, and Susan Stevens. 2005. *The Great Fuzz Frenzy*. Orlando, FL: Harcourt.

Stevenson, James. 1986. *When I Was Nine*. New York: Greenwillow.

———. 1996. *I Meant to Tell You*. New York: Greenwillow.

Stewart, Sarah. 1997. *The Gardener*. New York: Farrar, Straus and Giroux.

Taylor, Mildred. 1990. *Mississippi Bridge*. New York: Dial Books for Young Readers.

Tsuchiya, Yukio. 1988. *Faithful Elephants: A True Story of Animals, People and War*. Boston: Houghton Mifflin.

verDorn, Bethea. 1992. *Day Breaks*. New York: Arcade.

Viorst, Judith. (1969) 1988. *I'll Fix Anthony*. New York: Harper and Row.

Waber, Bernard. 2002. *Courage*. Boston: Houghton Mifflin.

Waddell, Martin. 1992. *Owl Babies*. Cambridge, MA: Candlewick.

Ward, Cindy. 1988. *Cookie's Week*. New York: Putnam.

White, Ruth. 1995. *Belle Prater's Boy*. New York: Farrar, Straus and Giroux.

Williams, Sherley Anne. 1992. *Working Cotton*. San Diego: Harcourt Brace.

Williams, Vera B. 1982. *A Chair for My Mother*. New York: Greenwillow.

Winter, Jeannette. 2006. *Mama*. Orlando, FL: Harcourt.

Wong, Janet S. 2000. *The Trip Back Home*. San Diego: Harcourt Brace.

Wood, Audrey. 2005. *King Bidgood's in the Bathtub*. Orlando, FL: Harcourt.

Woodson, Jacqueline. 2001. *The Other Side*. New York: Putnam's.

———. 2004. *Coming on Home Soon*. New York: G. P. Putnam's Sons.

Yolen, Jane. 1987. *Owl Moon*. New York: Philomel.

Yorinks, Arthur. 1980. *Louis the Fish*. New York: Farrar, Straus & Giroux.

Ziefert, Harriet. 2001. *39 Uses for a Friend*. New York: Putnam's.

———. 2005. *40 Uses for a Grandpa*. Maplewood, NJ: Blue Apple Books/ Chronicle.

Zolotow, Charlotte. 1963. *A Tiger Called Thomas*. New York: Lothrop, Lee and Shepard.

———. 1995. *The Old Dog*. New York: HarperCollins.

Qualities of Writing Index

IDEAS: The Writer Must Have Something to Say

DESIGN: Strong Writing Has an Overall Shape or Design

LANGUAGE: Well-Chosen Language Allows Ideas to Take Flight

References

Boyd, Blanche McCrary. 1990. In *Shoptalk: Learning to Write with Writers*, by Donald Murray. Portsmouth, NH: Boynton Cook/Heinemann.

Calkins, Lucy. 1986. *The Art of Teaching Writing*. Portsmouth, NH: Heinemann.

Elbow, Peter. 1981. *Writing with Power: Techniques for Mastering the Writing Process*. New York: Oxford University Press.

Fletcher, Ralph. 1996. *A Writer's Notebook: Unlocking the Writer Within You*. New York: HarperCollins.

Graves, Donald. 1978. *Balance the Basics: Let Them Write*. New York: Ford Foundation.

———. 1983. Writing: *Teachers and Children at Work*. Portsmouth, NH: Heinemann.

———. 1989. *Experiment with Fiction*. Portsmouth, NH: Heinemann.

———. 1994. *A Fresh Look at Writing*. Portsmouth, NH: Heinemann.

Heard, Georgia. 1989. *For the Good of the Earth and Sun: Teaching Poetry*. Portsmouth, NH: Heinemann.

Johnson, Pat. 2006. *One Child at a Time: Making the Most of Your Time with Struggling Readers, K–6*. Portland, ME: Stenhouse.

Lane, Barry. 1993. *After the End: Teaching and Learning Creative Revision*. Portsmouth, NH: Heinemann.

McPhee, John. 1965. *A Sense of Where You Are*. New York: Farrar, Straus and Giroux.

Murray, Donald. 1990. *Shoptalk: Learning to Write with Writers*. Portsmouth, NH: Boynton Cook/Heinemann.

———. 1993. *Write to Learn*. 4th ed. San Diego: Harcourt Brace.

———. 1996. *Crafting a Life in Essay, Story, Poem*. Portsmouth, NH: Boynton Cook/Heinemann.

Portalupi, JoAnn, and Ralph Fletcher. 2004. *Teaching the Qualities of Writing*. Portsmouth, NH: Heinemann.

Wilford, John Noble. 1997. "The Brightest Star Ever Seen." *New York Times*, 8 November.

Will, George F. 2007. "Barry Bonds's Enhancements." *Newsweek*, May 21.